www.wadsworth.com

wadsworth.com is the World Wide Web site for Wadsworth Publishing Company and is your direct source to dozens of online resources.

At *wadsworth.com* you can find out about supplements, demonstration software, and student resources. You can also send e-mail to many of our authors and preview new publications and exciting new technologies.

wadsworth.com
Changing the way the world learns®

TEACHER AS REFLECTIVE PRACTITIONER AND ACTION RESEARCHER

Richard D. Parsons
Kimberlee S. Brown
West Chester University

Wadsworth
Thomson Learning.

Australia • Canada • Mexico • Singapore • Spain
United Kingdom • United States

Education Editor: Dan Alpert
Associate Development Editor: Tangelique Williams
Editorial Assistant: Alex Orr
Marketing Manager: Becky Tollerson
Project Manager, Editorial Production: Trudy Brown
Print/Media Buyer: Robert King
Permissions Editor: Bob Kauser

Production, Illustration, and Composition:
    Summerlight Creative
Text Designer: Lisa Delgado
Copy Editor: Julia Defty
Cover Designer: Brenda Duke
Text and Cover Printer: Globus Printing

Wadsworth/Thomson Learning
10 Davis Drive
Belmont, CA 94002-3098
USA

For more information about our products, contact us:
Thomson Learning Academic Resource Center
1-800-423-0563
http://www.wadsworth.com

International Headquarters
Thomson Learning
International Division
290 Harbor Drive, 2nd Floor
Stamford, CT 06902-7477
USA

UK/Europe/Middle East/South Africa
Thomson Learning
Berkshire House
168-173 High Holborn
London WC1V 7AA
United Kingdom

Asia
Thomson Learning
60 Albert Street, #15-01
Albert Complex
Singapore 189969

Canada
Nelson Thomson Learning
1120 Birchmount Road
Toronto, Ontario M1K 5G4
Canada

Library of Congress
Cataloging-in-Publication Data

Parsons, Richard D.
    Teacher as reflective practitioner and action researcher / Richard Parsons, Kimberlee Brown.
        p. cm.
    Includes bibliographical references and index.
    ISBN 0-534-55711-2
    1. Action research in education. I. Brown, Kimberlee. II. Title.

LB1028.24 .P34 2001
371.102—dc21

For Kristian, Drew, and Jonathan—three sons who would make any dad very proud, and who make this dad simply burst with joy.

—Rick Parsons

To my Dad, whose love and strength continues to anchor my life, and to my son, Ben, whose smile gives meaning and purpose to my life.

—Kim Brown

CONTENTS

Prologue

The classroom can be a place of energy, excitement, and wonderment. However, these classroom characteristics do not happen simply by chance. They are the results of the knowledge, skills, and reflective decision making of a professional educator. The teacher is engaged in many decisions, including determining *what* to teach, *when* to teach it, and *how* to teach it. The teacher makes numerous decisions about classroom arrangement and how to respond to any one child at any one particular time.

Interacting with so many individuals, around so many crucial issues, requires that the teacher know what needs to be accomplished, the options available for accomplishing those goals, and then deciding on which option to employ in order to facilitate the learning process. The question that must also be answered, however, is, "Was the decision a good, effective decision?"

TEACHERS AS REFLECTIVE PRACTITIONERS

In *The Reflective Practitioner* (1983), Donald Schön describes teaching as an activity filled with uncertainty and one so complicated that teachers cannot merely apply what they have learned in an unsystematic manner. Rather, teachers need to reflect "in" and "on" their action and make adaptations based on their own unique situations. There are very few specific guides or "how-to" books to assist this decision-making process. Although teachers can call upon a growing database of research and well-formulated theory to aid in their decision making, theory and research need to be translated and applied to each unique teaching situation. To be effective, a teacher must be an active participant in the classroom and an observer of the learning process, analyzing and interpreting the information presented within the classroom and using that information, along with the more classic theory and research, as a base for planning and decision making.

The ability to interpret classroom activity to make instructional and classroom management decisions is a characteristic of "expert" teachers. (Berliner 1987; Borko & Shavelson, 1990; Carter et al., 1987). This process of developing lessons with thoughtful consideration of educational theory and research, along with the analysis of the plan's effect on the students' learning, has been called **reflective teaching** (Schön, 1983; Cruickshank, 1987).

TEACHERS AS ACTION RESEARCHERS

Most teachers who attempt to be reflective often rely on their memories of events or perhaps use casual observations, which are nonsystematic. If these observations are to provide meaningful data and useful guidance, they need to be systematic and valid. Systematic observations and data collection help transform reflection into **action research** (Casanova, 1989; Cochran-Smith & Lytle, 1990). Action research methodology provides teachers with the means of acquiring valid, useful data, which in turn can be used for the development of effective strategies of professional practice. Although interest in and examples of action research have been on the rise (e.g., Casanova, 1989; Cochran-Smith & Lytle, 1990), texts providing teachers with useful models of action research are noticeably absent. This text fills the void between the idea of action research as a valuable tool and the specifics of transforming a reflective teacher into a practitioner and action researcher.

TEXT STRUCTURE AND ORGANIZATION

The text emphasizes *application* and *practice*. However, even with this "practical" focus, each of the following chapters provides a blending of theory and practice, as well as a brief description of research constructs and models as applied to classroom issues. The chapters provide numerous illustrations of the application of these constructs and models within the classroom setting. Finally, each chapter will engage the reader in the application of specific action research methods by way of simulated case illustrations and directed learning activities.

Each chapter will include:

- ◆ Objectives
- ◆ A specific principle or method of research
- ◆ A specific teaching strategy, concept or decision point for which the research principle or method has special value
- ◆ Case illustrations: Blending the teaching concept with the research principle within the classroom setting
- ◆ Cooperative Learning exercises
- ◆ Individual guided practice exercise
- ◆ Connections: Internet linkage

◆ Key terms

◆ Suggested readings

CHAPTER OVERVIEW

Chapter 1 provides an overview to the teacher as reflective practitioner and action researcher. In addition to defining the "what" and "why" of action research, the chapter assists the reader in understanding the fundamental elements of the action research process. Though the focus of the text is on practical application, Chapter 2 emphasizes the fundamental scientific principles of action research. In this chapter, the reader will begin to conceptualize action research as more than soft science by discussing the principles of research and the threats to the validity when fundamentals are not observed.

Section II focuses on the application of specific action research principles and methods to the study of student characteristics and the effect of those principles on teacher decision making. The section highlights the value of reflective teaching and action research as applied to the understanding of the special resources, limitations, and instructional opportunities encountered as a function of the student's normative level of cognitive (Chapter 3), psycho-social, and moral development (Chapter 4) and their individual social, cultural, and personal variations (Chapters 5 and 6).

The focus of Section III is on the use of research design and control to more fully assess the impact of the teacher's decision to incorporate behavioral learning theory (Chapter 7), cognitive learning theory (Chapter 8), and motivational theory (Chapter 9) within the classroom. Section IV, "Becoming an Action Researcher," guides the reader through the entire process of action research. The reader will be assisted in applying the previous material to a case study and to their own work experience (Chapter 10). The text ends with an epilogue, which reinforces both the utility of action research for practice and the professional responsibility of every teacher to become an action researcher.

ACKNOWLEDGMENTS

We would like to thank the following reviewers for their helpful suggestions during the preparation of this manuscript: Stephen Brand, University of Rhode Island; Barbara Kawulich, Georgia State University; Kris Montis, Lake Superior State University; John Nietfield, State

University of West Georgia; and Dawn Shinew, Washington State University.

AN INVITATION

As you read this text and begin to use action research methods in your teaching, you will note an increase in both the validity and utility of your professional decisions. We invite you to share your experiences, your insights, and your findings with us. We also invite you to respond to this text and help shape it through your feedback. Are there points that you found particularly helpful? Are there area that seemed less than clear or helpful? Do you have suggestions that may benefit future readers? Do you have your own action research or reflections from the field you would like to share? Please send your letters to R. Parsons and K. Brown at Wadsworth/Thomson Learning, 10 Davis Drive, Belmont, CA 94002.

Rick Parsons

Kimberlee Brown

West Chester, Pennsylvania

REFERENCES

Berliner, C. D. (1987) Ways of thinking about students and classrooms by more and less experienced teachers. In J. Calderhead (Ed.), *Exploring teacher's thinking.* London: Cassell Educational Limited.

Borko, H., & Shavelson, R. J. (1990). Teacher's decision making. In B. Jones & L. Idols (Eds.), *Dimensions of thinking and cognitive instruction.* Hillsdale, NJ: Erlbaum.

Carter, K., Sabers, D., Cushing, K., Pinnegar, S., & Berliner, D. (1987). Processing and using information about students: A study of expert, novice and postulant teachers. *Teaching and Teacher Education, 3*(2), 147–157.

Casanova, V. (1989). Research and practice—we can integrate them. *N.E.A. Today, 7*(6), 44–49.

Cochran-Smith, M., & Lytle, S. L. (1990). Research on teaching and teacher research: The issues that divide. *Education Researchers, 19*(2),2–10.

Cruickshank, D. (1987). *Reflective teaching: The preparation of students of teaching.* Reston, VA: Association of Teacher Education.

Schön, D. (1983). *The reflective practitioner: How professionals think in action.* San Francisco: Jossey-Bass.

ACTION RESEARCH: INCREASING EFFECTIVENESS OF TEACHER DECISION MAKING

CHAPTER 1

Teachers as Reflective Practitioners and Action Researchers

Okay, so I have all of the students in their cooperative learning groups and I developed really neat material. Why aren't they interacting?

The teacher in the introductory scenario is demonstrating one of the many "realities of the classroom." Although one might be enthused about using a specific teaching strategy such as a cooperative learning structure (Johnson & Johnson, 1994; Slavin, 1995), the reality is that sometimes a theory, a concept, or an approach, while well founded, must be adjusted to account for the unique characteristics of the situation to which it is applied. Do the facts that a teacher's class is a middle-school class and the students are in mixed-gender groups make a difference in the use of a cooperative learning structure? Or is it possible that because many of her students are of Asian American heritage, they affect the group dynamic?

Adapting a theory, or even a standard of practice, in response to the unique characteristics of the setting or population with whom the practice is employed can result in its increased utility and effectiveness. Further, when such adaptation is conceived and implemented with the rigors of scientific research, the resulting data can lead to the increased refinement and validity of the underlying theory. This systematic adjustment of theory to practice and of theory from practice lies at the heart of **action research.**

◆ Chapter Objectives

The value of teachers acting as reflective practitioners and action researchers is the focus of the current chapter. A review of the current literature highlighting definitions, implications, and sample applications of action research is provided.

After reading this chapter, you should be able to do the following:

1 Define action research.

2 Describe the utility of a reflective approach to classroom teaching.

3 Provide examples of potential targets for action research within an educational setting.

REFLECTIVE PRACTITIONER AND ACTION RESEARCHER

As noted in the Prologue, **reflective teachers** know what they are doing and why they decided to do it, and then review the effect of what was done. Quite often, a teacher fails to approach teaching from a reflective stance. Without **systematic reflection** of practice decisions, teachers may find themselves doing what Judith McGonigal describes in her autobiographical case study: "unthinkingly [teaching] the prescribed curriculum the same passive way for 15 years" (1999, p. 5).

◆ From Reflection to Action Research

Schon (1983) claimed that important decisions are made during the act of teaching and that most often these decisions are based primarily on experience in a spontaneous, intuitive manner. Although **reflection** is a valued quality of effective teachers, even when based on nonsystematic memories of events or casual observations, the value of reflection is increased when based on data collected through **systematic observations** and data collection procedures (Lederman & Niess, 1997). When teachers employ systematic approaches to observations and data collection, they move into the realm of action researcher (Casanova, 1989; Cochran-Smith & Lytle, 1990; Hovda & Kyle, 1984).

Action research has been broadly defined (e.g., Goode & Bartunek, 1990; Peters & Robinson, 1984; Shani, 1990) as a form of investigation that enables teachers to examine their own practices (Tomlinson, 1995). As presented here, action research is **applied research** in which the researcher/investigator is also the practitioner (i.e., teacher) and attempts to *use research as a methodology for identifying the "what" they do and make decisions on doing it better.*

Action research goes beyond simple common sense. **Teachers as action researchers** apply the rigors of **scientific inquiry** in the context of their classroom and classroom experience in an attempt to improve teaching effectiveness. Because action research is conducted by classroom teachers, it serves as a vehicle through which teachers investigate issues of interest and then incorporate the results into their own planning and future teaching.

◆ Action Research: It's Everywhere!

A quick perusal of an educational psychology text (e.g., Parsons, Hinson & Brown, 2001) might imply that action research is one of the latest "in" topics, with a short life span as a professional practice. Although action research is currently receiving a lot of attention among educators, it is far from a new or short-lived approach to professional practice. In fact, the concept of teacher as researcher was discussed in the 1920s (Buckingham, 1926). Further, the use of action research within the classroom has been in evidence since the early 1950s (Zeichner & Gore, 1995). As will be highlighted below, action research has been on the rise

CONTENT MAP 1

(Casanova, 1989; Cochran-Smith & Lytle, 1990) and has been employed as an approach for facilitating educational changes within a classroom, throughout a school, and across districts.

Action research is part of a teacher's professional life and will endure as long as teachers desire to improve their effectiveness and maintain their professionalism.

REFLECTIVE PRACTITIONER AND ACTION RESEARCHER: WHY?

Mention the word *research* to many teachers and you may encounter looks of confusion or concern and even gasps of horror! For many, the concept of research conjures images of large samples, complicated designs, and sophisticated statistical and computer analyses. Many teachers feel that they lack the necessary skills and the necessary drive and desire to become researchers, "action" or otherwise. So why should they? What possibly could be the draw?

Research and practice are not mutually exclusive. Rather, they are necessary for a teacher's continued professional growth, and research can ensure the efficacy of practice decisions. However, large-scale research projects are often prohibitive to the classroom teacher because they may require sophisticated, oftentimes elaborate designs for data collection and analysis. But action research, as presented here, is a mind-set as much as it is a method. It is a way of approaching teaching with a desire to be accountable for professional practice and motivated by the desire to improve such service. Action research provides teachers with a method for viewing their professional decisions systematically and deciding on them rationally.

In addition to providing a vehicle for improving teacher decision making and increasing teacher effectiveness, an action research approach to professional practice can be used to explore a variety of issues in education. For example, Calhoun (1993) suggested that action research can (1) be a tool for the individual teacher focusing on changes within his or her classroom, (2) be an approach employed by a "research team" of teachers addressing a problem that extends across classrooms, and (3) be a facilitative approach to schoolwide or districtwide problems.

◆ Improving Practice

Action research is a model of research that has, as its focus, the improvement of practice. It is a model that guides the teacher in making practical decisions about, or improvements in, his or her teaching strategies. From this perspective, the strength of action research rests in the fact that it is self-evaluative and collaborative and ultimately will lead to an improvement in practice.

As teachers, we may want to believe that we have mastered our professions. The truth is that we need to reflect on our actions and the consequences of those actions. The need to reflect and continue to acquire knowledge and improve practice is clear. Each situation, each class, each student provides unique challenges and opportunities, and each calls from us unique approaches. Systematic reflection on our teaching at any one time can provide the impetus and means for improving practice.

Reflective teachers approach their classes with the belief that change can occur and that they can effect that change. They seek those strategies that will assist them in becoming most effective. It is in this process of reflecting on what was done—what resulted and then asking the question "What if?"—and implementing those innovations that the reflective practitioner becomes the action researcher (Bennett, 1994).

◆ A Tool for Professional Development

Action research has been found to serve not only as a means of improving teaching (e.g., Elliott, 1991; Nixon, 1987) but also in developing practitioners' flexibility and problem-solving skills (Pine, 1981) and their attitudes to professional development and the process of change (Simmons, 1985). Participation in action research resulted in increased confidence, self-esteem, willingness to embrace research, and liberated creative potential for the educator-turned-action researcher (McKay, 1992). These findings indicate that educators grow personally and professionally as an outgrowth of employing action research. Beyond the benefit to the individual teacher, action research has been described as a vehicle for improving preservice teacher education (Noffke & Stevenson, 1995), in-service teacher education (Letiche, van der Wolf, & Plooij, 1991), and for ongoing staff development (Miller & Pine,1990). Further, the sharing of professional experiences has been found to promote a climate of professionalism and scholarship (Allen & Shockley, 1994).

◆ Increasing the Utility of Practice and the Validity of Research

Action research challenges the common wisdom and shared perspective that research occurs within the ivory towers, whereas practice takes place in the trenches. This perspective presents practitioners as consumers who apply the findings of the researcher. Hoshmand and Polkinghorne (1992) noted that the traditional concept of the relationship between science and practice has generally posited a one-way influence of science on practice. This perspective is limiting and underutilizes and undervalues the ways of knowing that are germane to practice. Action research brings those two realms of knowledge and experience together.

Like most research, action research involves research questions and hypotheses. The teacher attempts to understand the current situation by speculating about the nature of the problems encountered and possible actions to be taken that will lead to improvements. In action research these actions will be implemented, and data depicting their impact will be collected, reviewed, and employed to improve the understanding of the problem. In this way, teaching decisions are not only shaped by theory and research, but in turn help give shape and new directions to educational theory and research.

◆ Social Action and Policy Making

Although the origin of action research is open for debate, many have placed it with the work of Kurt Lewin (1946). A primary target for Lewin's writing and work on action research was the need to close the gap between social action and social theory (Peters & Robinson, 1984). He viewed action research as a tool for generating knowledge about a social system while at the same time attempting to change it (Lewin, 1946).

McLean described action research as a "process of systematically evaluating the consequences of educational decisions and adjusting practice to maximize effectiveness" (McLean, 1995, p 3.). McKay, for example, suggested that action research can be used to investigate a variety of organizational practices, such as the implementation of a K–8 or K–5 and 7–8 grade alignment, or the value of interdisciplinary or departmentalized school structures (McKay, 1992).

Thus, action research can assist educators with a systematic method for determining what is best practice and policy for their students and can promote educational reform (Heckman, 1996; Zuber-Skerritt, 1991).

◆ Action Research: An Ethical Consideration

Viewed as a frame of mind, action research calls us to a continued interest in serving our students better and providing increased accountability for our teaching. As such, action research is not simply a good idea. Rather, it becomes an ethical responsibility for monitoring the effectiveness of our practice and increasing the competency of our teaching. Elliott (1991) suggests that action research applied to education is an ethical process that integrates

> teaching and teacher development, curriculum development and evaluation, research and philosophical reflection, into a unified conception of reflective educational practice. (Elliot, 1991, p. 54)

No one professional can guarantee success in each and every encounter or situation. However, ethical teachers need to assess the degree to which their teaching decisions and strategies are both valid and effective. Action research provides a mechanism for monitoring the efficacy and adequacy of practice decisions and methods.

So why use action research? Because, as will become evident as you read the case applications in the upcoming chapters, action research is a vehicle for improving classroom practice, teacher knowledge and skill, and the overall functioning and performance of our educational systems.

THE ACTION RESEARCH PROCESS

The typical conceptualization of action research is that it is a **cyclical inquiry process** that involves identifying and defining a problem, developing action steps as a way of resolving the problem or improving the situation, implementing those action steps, and then evaluating the outcomes (Elden & Chisholm, 1993). Case Illustration 1-1 provides an example of this cyclical process of inquiry.

As suggested by the example, an action researcher engages in a process of observing-doing-observing-adjusting and doing again. Action research can take many forms and employ a wide range of methodologies. The key to a worthwhile teacher-initiated investigation lies not in the methodology used, or the types of data collected, but in the questions researched and the degree to which they are meaningful and important to the teacher (Spaudling, 1992).

Throughout the following chapters examples of action research will be presented. In each example, it is clear that the teacher, as action researcher, is primarily concerned with documenting the effectiveness of a particular program or procedure employed within the classroom, as

Case Illustration 1-1
Jerome: A Ninth-Grade English Teacher

Jerome is a first-year, ninth-grade English teacher. Jerome noted that he was having difficulty getting his students to engage in class discussion about the assigned readings. He felt that he has been encouraging and nonevaluative and has provided the students with stimulating "Questions for Reflection." However, getting class discussion is almost "like pulling teeth."

Jerome shared his frustration with Ginny, his team partner, who taught the same students in science and mathematics. Ginny suggested that perhaps the classroom structure may in some way be inhibiting the open discussion. Ginny shared her own experience of teaching science principles and then attempting to have the students discuss the relevance of those principles in their lives. She noted that moving from a lecture to a discussion format was difficult for the students until she rearranged the seating configuration in her classroom. Ginny shared what she had discovered through reading and experience—that discussions seemed to increase when the students were placed in a semicircle arrangement. Ginny gave Jerome an article by three educational researchers (Rosenfield, Lambert, & Black, 1985), which demonstrated that a semicircular seating arrangement (as opposed to straight rows) facilitated face-to-face communication, and thus increased spontaneous interaction among students.

Jerome liked the idea and decided to try an *experiment* using his two sections of English Literature. In

one section he decided to rearrange his classroom seating, moving the chairs from a single-row, front-facing arrangement to a large-circle arrangement with the teacher as a member of the circle. For his second session, he maintained the teacher-focused structure of straight-row seating.

As a way of assessing the impact of this seating option, Jerome took notes on how many of the ten stimulus questions he needed to use to elicit discussion during the twenty-minute discussion period. He *hypothesized* that with increased student participation about each question, fewer questions would be used. Following two weeks of running his experiment, Jerome reviewed his recorded data. He found that when the classroom was arranged in a circular formation the students required, on average, only three of the stimulus questions to start the twenty-minute discussion session during the daily class periods. However, in the group in which the classroom was arranged in straight rows, facing the teacher's desk, students went through eight of the stimulus questions during the same twenty-minute period.

From this experience, Jerome decided to arrange his rooms to allow for both teacher-directed (straight-row arrangement) and large-group discussion (circle arrangement). He even decided to read more about the impact of the "ecology" of the classroom on student learning (Parsons, Hinson, & Brown, 2001).

Action Research

Secondary Science Education

As noted above, action research is an important way to both increase the effectiveness of classroom practices and stimulate improvement of overall functioning within an entire school.

Consider the following example of a preservice secondary science teacher, Caroline, concerned with identifying effective strategies in teaching science to linguistically diverse students (Keating, Diaz-Greenberg, Baldwin, & Thousand, 1998).

Caroline was interested in "investigating" the use and effectiveness of a specific science technique, the Specially Designed Academic Instruction in English (SDAIE), by a particular group of science teachers. Specifically, Caroline wanted to investigate:

1. How this approach differed from approaches used in mainstream classes
2. The difference in material taught in those classes compared with mainstream classes
3. Variation in the use of that strategy among science teachers
4. The effectiveness of SDAIE strategies related to student interest and achievement in science.

Method

Caroline used observations, interviews, and questionnaires with the three teachers employing SDAIE, as well as interviews and questionnaires from a selected group of students enrolled in three SDAIE classes.

Results

The data collected revealed the following trends:

1. There was a distinctiveness in the strategies used in SDAIE classes when compared with the mainstream science classes.
2. Although the amount of time spent on SDAIE strategies varied among the three teachers, all three teachers employed specific SDAIE strategies (e.g., using multi-modalities in delivering instruction, using student-centered activities).
3. The teachers covered fewer topics in these classes compared with the mainstream science classes. However, more depth of coverage was observed.
4. Students appeared to have increased understanding and achievement and expressed a more positive attitude toward science.

Conclusion

This preservice teacher concluded that the use of SDAIE strategies was very effective with linguistically diverse students. Sharing her data with her master teacher increased the master teacher's interest in the use of an action research approach to evaluating educational classroom questions.

opposed to developing a new theory or publishing a research paper. However, even with this emphasis on application as opposed to theory building, this informal classroom-based research should be coherent and systematic and should provide valuable information for the teacher. The steps described in the remaining chapters will assist the teacher as practitioner to incorporate the perspective and rigor of the researcher into her daily practice in order to increase both her awareness of the "what she does" and the effectiveness of her decisions on "how to do it better"!

COOPERATIVE LEARNING EXERCISES

Increasing Awareness of Teaching Decisions

As a teacher you probably feel that you do not have the time or resources to perform research. As suggested throughout this chapter, action research is as much a matter of mind as it is a matter of method. Becoming an action researcher may require little more than becoming aware of your practice decisions and their impact. Simply becoming more reflective of what you do, why you did it, and what results from it is key to being an action researcher.

Working with Your Classmates or Colleagues

Step 1. Identify three decisions that you might make in the course of your professional day. For example, you may decide to introduce a new concept to the students by showing a brief movie or perhaps at some time you may choose to ignore a child who is calling out in order to receive attention. Identify three such strategies for your professional practice.

Step 2. Select one of those strategies that you feel you would continue to implement in your teaching.

Step 3. Select two very specific impacts or outcomes you would expect from such an action. In other words, what were you hoping to accomplish and how would it look if it were accomplished? Be as concrete as possible.

Step 4. Assuming that your goal was met, how could you demonstrate it? What type of evidence would you use to show the impact of your action?

Step 5. Return to your three strategies and select one of the remaining two. Follow Steps 3 and 4 to examine their effectiveness.

INDIVIDUAL GUIDED PRACTICE EXERCISE

Targeting an Area for Action Research

The following exercise is provided in an attempt to help you personalize the materials just presented. In this exercise, you will be asked to observe, conceptualize, and reflect on a potential area of concern that may benefit from action research.

Step 1. Select a classroom teacher and simply make observations about the teacher's decisions and behaviors during a defined time frame (e.g., 30 minutes).

Step 2. Attempt to identify a potential problem being exhibited by one or more students in that setting. For example, are there any children not attending to the teacher?

Step 3. Keep detailed notes describing how the teacher is addressing this specific problem. Did the teacher go over to the inattentive student? Did the teacher verbally reprimand the student?

Step 4. Collect data that might reflect on the impact or effect of the teacher's actions. How did the student respond? How about other students?

Step 5. Using your description of the problem area, the steps implemented by the teacher, and the apparent impact, identify an alternative set of action steps you may have implemented or would implement at this stage of the process. What is the basis (e.g., theoretical, empirical, or experiential) for your decision?

Directions

Using a search engine or portal such as yahoo.com (Yahoo), lycos.com (Lycos), or av.com (Alta Vista), search the following terms:

- ◆ reflective teaching
- ◆ action research

Simply scan the resources that are brought to your attention as a way of beginning to understand the value and general acceptance of those approaches to teaching. Begin to create a list of professional exchanges or web sites that you could visit at a later time.

Connections

In this and all of the remaining chapters you will be invited to "surf the net" and make connections. The Internet allows you to connect not just with a wealth of information, but also with a vast pool of other professionals.

The exercises presented in the Connections section of each chapter are designed to expand and enrich the material presented within the chapter. Further, these exercises are created to provide you with the opportunity to connect with professionals who, like you, are reflective in practice and in pursuit of information and strategies that will increase their classroom effectiveness.

◆ Key Terms

action research

applied research

cyclical inquiry process

reflection

reflective teacher

scientific inquiry

systematic observations

systematic reflection

teacher as action researcher

◆ Suggested Readings

Anderson, L. W., & Burns, R. B. (1989). *Research in the classrooms: The study of teachers, teaching and instruction.* New York: Pergamon.

Bogdan, R. C., & Biklen, S. K. (1998). *Qualitative research in education: An introduction to theory and methods.* Boston: Allyn & Bacon.

Elliott, J. (1991). *Action research for educational change.* Philadelphia: Open University Press.

Valli, L. (1997). Listening to other voices: A description of teacher reflection in the United States. *Peabody Journal of Education, 72*(1), 67–88.

◆ References

Allen, J., & Shockley, D. (1994). *Becoming a community of researchers.* Paper presented at the annual meeting of the American Educational Research Association.

Bennett, C. K. (1994). Promoting teacher reflection through action research: What do teachers think? *Journal of Staff Development, 15*(1), 34–38.

Buckingham, B. R. (1926). *Research for teachers.* New York: Silver, Burdette & Co.

Calhoun, E. F. (1993). Action research: Three approaches. *Educational Leadership, 51*(2), 62–65.

Casanova, V. (1989). Research and practice—We can integrate them. *NEA Today, 7*(6), 44–49.

Cochran-Smith, M., & Lytle, S. L. (1990). Research on teaching and teacher research: The issues that divide. *Education Researchers, 19*(2), 2–10.

Elden, M., & Chisholm, R. F. (1993). Emerging varieties of action research: Introduction to the special issue. *Human Relations, 46*(2), 121–142.

Elliott, J. (1991). *Action research for educational change.* Philadelphia: Open University Press.

Goode, L., & Bartunek, J. (1990). Action research in an underbounded setting. *Consultation, 9*(3), 209–228.

Heckman, P. E. (1996). *The courage to change: Stories from successful school reform.* Thousand Oaks, CA: Corwin.

Hoshmand, L. T., & Polkinghorne, D. E. (1992). Defining the science–practice relationship and professional training. *American Psychologist, 47*(1), 55–66.

Hovda, R., & Kyle, D. (1984). Action research: A professional development possibility. *Middle School Journal, 15*(3), 21–23.

Johnson, D., & Johnson, R. (1994). *Learning together and alone: Cooperation, competition and individualization* (4th ed.). Boston: Allyn & Bacon.

Keating, J., Diaz-Greenberg, R., Baldwin, M., & Thousand, J. (1998). A collaborative action research model for teacher preparation programs. *Journal of Teacher Education, 49*(5), 381–390.

Lederman, N. G., & Niess, M. L. (1997). Action research: Our actions may speak louder than our words. *School Science and Mathematics, 97*(8), 397–399.

Letiche, H. K., van der Wolf, J. C., & Plooij, F. X. (Eds.) (1991). *The practitioner's power of choice in staff development and in-service training.* Lisse, Netherlands: Swets & Zeitlinger.

Lewin, K. (1946). Action research and minority problems. *Journal of Social Issues, 2*(1), 65.

McGonigal, J. A. (1999). How learning to become a teacher-researcher prepared an educator to do Science

Inquiry with elementary grade students. *Research in Science Education, 29*(1), 5–23.

McKay, J. A. (1992). Professional development through action research. *Journal of Staff Development, 13*(1), 18–21.

McLean, J. E. (1995). *Improving education through action research: A guide for administrators and teachers.* Thousand Oaks, CA: Corwin Press.

Miller, D. M., & Pine, G. J. (1990). Advancing professional inquiry for educational improvement through action research. *Journal of Staff Development, 11*(3), 56–61.

Nixon, J. (1987). The teacher as researcher: Contradictions and continuities. *Peabody Journal of Education, 64*(2), 20–32.

Noffke, S. E., & Stevenson, R. B. (Eds.). (1995). *Educational action research: Becoming practically critical.* New York: Teacher College Press.

Parsons, R. D., Hinson, S., & Brown, D. (2001). *Educational psychology: A practitioner-researcher model of teaching.* Belmont, CA: Wadsworth.

Peters, M., & Robinson, V. (1984). The origins and status of action research. *Journal of Applied Behavioral Science, 20*(2), 113–124.

Pine, G. J. (1981). *Collaborative action research: The integration of research and service.* Paper presented at the Annual Meeting of the American Association of Colleges for Teacher Education (Detroit, MI, February).

Rosenfield, P., Lambert, S., & Black, R. (1985). Desk arrangement effects on pupil classroom behavior. *Journal of Educational Psychology, 77*, 101–108.

Sardo-Brown, D. (1990). Middle level teachers' perceptions of action research. *Middle School Journal, 22*(3), 30–32.

Schon, D. A. (1983). *Educating the reflective practitioner.* San Francisco: Jossey-Bass.

Shani, A. B. (1990). Solving problems bureaucracies cannot handle. In G. Bushe & A. B. Shani (Eds.), *Parallel learning structures.* Reading, MA: Addison-Wesley.

Simmons, J. M. (1985). *Exploring the relationship between research & practice: The impact of assuming the role of action researcher in one's own classroom.* Paper presented at the 69th Annual Meeting of the American Educational Research Association (Chicago, IL, March 31–April 4).

Slavin, R. E. (1995). *Cooperative learning* (2nd ed.). Boston: Allyn & Bacon.

Spaudling, C. L. (1992). *Motivation in the classroom.* New York: McGraw-Hill.

Tomlinson, C. S. (1995). Action research and practical inquiry: An overview. *Journal for the Education of the Gifted, 18*(4) 467–484.

Zeichner, K., & Gore, J. (1995). Using action research as a vehicle for student teacher reflection: A social reconstructionist approach. Pp. 13–30 in S. Noffke & R. Stevenson (Eds.), *Educational action research: Becoming practically critical.* New York: Teachers College Press.

Zuber-Skerritt, O. (Ed.). (1991). *Action research for change and development.* Brookfield, VT: Avebury.

CHAPTER 2

The Fundamentals Still Apply

I'm pretty good at observing the kids as they interact or react to me in the class. I even write things down and try to think about it before I make changes. I just never feel totally confident that what I am seeing is accurate or that the conclusions I draw are valid.

CONTENT MAP 2

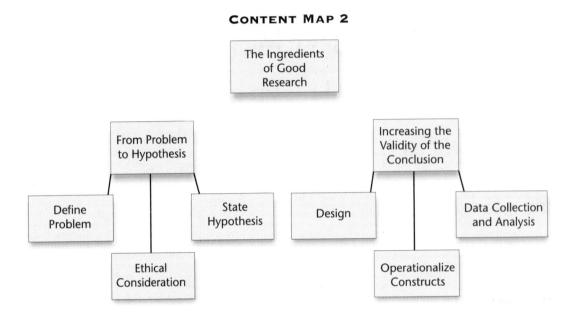

The teacher cited above is certainly aware of the value of a reflective approach to teaching. As noted in Chapter 1, observing, reflecting, and adjusting are all important elements of being a reflective teacher. In addition to demonstrating the process of reflection in teaching, this teacher articulates an additional concern: How can teachers be confident that what they observe and what they conclude from these observations are correct?

Moving from simply being reflective to becoming more systematic in observations and reflections increases the ability to draw valid conclusions from observations. Using the fundamentals of research as guides to reflective teaching increases the validity of teachers' conclusions and moves the teacher into the role of action researcher.

Whether it's known as participatory or applied, action research is still research. Teachers functioning as action researchers will benefit from the application of research fundamentals in their professional practice.

◆ Chapter Objectives

The current chapter highlights the fundamentals of good research. The chapter discusses how teachers as action researchers can incorporate those fundamentals into their own teaching, ensuring the *research* in "action research," and thereby increasing the accuracy of the observations made and the conclusions drawn. In addition, the chapter identifies the necessary steps the teachers as practitioner-researchers must take in order to increase the validity of their research and practice.

After reading this chapter, the reader should be able to do the following:

1 Redefine an observation into a researchable question and that question into a testable hypothesis.

2 Describe methods of data collection and analysis for both qualitative and quantitative research.

THE INGREDIENTS OF GOOD RESEARCH

In an attempt to improve practice, the teacher as practitioner-researcher must move from simply recognizing and defining a problem or an area of interest to actually planning and implementing a strategy for approaching the problem. Further, as researchers, teachers need to gather data and analyze those findings as a means of assessing the effectiveness of the particular practice under review. Teachers as practitioner-researchers must include the basic ingredients of research methodology in their practice strategies. These basic ingredients are:

1. Defining the Problem: What needs to be improved or developed? Action researchers select problems that engage their attention. They have a true desire to find solutions to those problems.

2. Reviewing the Literature: What have others found about this situation? The action researcher seeks insights into the problem and possible solutions by reviewing existing research.

3. Stating the Hypothesis: What does the action researcher expect to find? The action researcher moves from simply wondering or posing questions to making predictions about what could happen.

4. Developing and Implementing a Design: What procedures or conditions will the action researcher use to meet the objectives and increase the validity of the findings?

5. Collecting and Analyzing Data: What techniques will the action researcher employ to gather feedback on the impact of the practices? What form of data will the action researcher collect and how will the data be analyzed?

Before discussing these elements in greater detail, an example illustrating how they may appear in a classroom situation will be presented (see Case Illustration 2-1).

Although the previous example is oversimplified, it highlights the potential benefit of framing the practice of teaching with a research

Case Illustration 2-1
Adjusting Teaching in Response to Cognitive Style

Mrs. L., a tenth-grade social studies teacher, often employed a process of reviewing material and providing practice oral testing in preparation for a major test. In reflecting on the students' participation in those oral review sessions, she concluded that some students appeared to react quickly and respond to the question almost immediately (observation). Further, she was aware that she would often call on these students. She wondered if those students who were less active were also less sure of the answers, or more confused about the material (testable question). After reviewing the literature on cognitive learning styles (Kagan, 1964) (reviewing the literature), she predicted that the students who were not responding quickly were just as knowledgeable as the quick responders. She thought it was possible that those students simply approached learning from a more reflective orientation (hypothesis). Mrs. L. identified the students who responded rapidly and those who took more time to respond and compared their average test scores (data collection and analysis). The data indicated that there were no consistent differences in test scores between those two groups of students. She then implemented a change in her process of reviewing for upcoming tests. She began using two different formats—a speed round in which questions and answers were presented in a rapid-fire format and a second format, which she labeled "a time-to-consider round." In this second form, when questions were asked, students were required to wait one full minute before responding (strategy). She noted during the time-to-consider round that more students (including those who previously did not participate) began to volunteer answers.

mind-set or perspective. Integrating the fundamentals of research with practice can lead to the *enhancement of the teacher's level of effectiveness.*

FROM PROBLEM TO HYPOTHESIS

♦ Define the Problem

Teachers acting as reflective practitioners seek to investigate issues that help shape decision making and classroom practice. This interest or curiosity may evolve from reading about a theory or from an experience encountered within the classroom. For example, Lisa, a tenth-grade science teacher, just attended a workshop on aggression in the schools, which highlighted the effects of culture and modeling of aggression on student behavior. As a result of the information received, she began to wonder if there were elements within her classroom or even within her school's culture that support or even model aggression for the children. In this case, curiosity and an area of interest was stimulated by the introduction of a new piece of information or theory. Rob, a fifth-grade language arts teacher, noticed that he seemed to make fewer referrals to the counselor's office for aggressive behavior than his partner, Al. Rob knew that Al maintained a very "tight ship" and was quick to punish the children for any violation of class rules, whereas Rob, who used more of a collaborative approach to rule formulation, discussed violations with his students first, before simply administering consequences. Rob started to wonder if the style and climate of those two classrooms somehow contributed to the level of aggression exhibited by the students.

Although both Lisa and Rob developed an interest in the impact of class climate on aggression, they came to this interest through different avenues. For Lisa it was theory that stimulated her interests; for Rob it was his personal experience. Theory and practice will serve as the two major sources for the action researcher's inquiry.

Once the action researcher has established an area of interest, the next step in defining the problem is to pose a **researchable question** (not just observe the problem). Moving from the "I wonder?" or "what if?" stage to developing a researchable question can be challenging. It is when reflective practitioners ask research-type questions that they begin to become action researchers (Bogdan & Biklen, 1998).

There are a number of ways in which research questions can be categorized. Drew (1980) suggested three general categories of research questions: descriptive, difference, and relationship. The first category, descriptive, includes questions that simply ask what "something is like." For example, the teacher who asks, "What goes on in a class that uses a cooperative goal structure?" is posing a **descriptive question.** A second form of questioning is the **difference question.** Difference questions are comparison questions that look at the differences between two or more phenomena. A teacher may be interested in knowing if students in a class employing cooperative learning strategies have different levels of achievement than those in a teacher-directed classroom. Finally, questions that explore the degree to which two or more constructs are related would be considered **relationship questions.** For example, the teacher in the previous example, having noticed differences in levels of achievement, may question the degree to which there is a relationship between the use of cooperative learning strategies and academic achievement. In order to examine those research questions, the researcher must frame them into a researchable format.

Kerlinger (1986) identified three criteria of "researchable" questions. First, a research question asks a question in a clear, unambiguous form. Secondly, the question asked focuses on a relationship between two or more constructs. Finally, the relationship is one that can be measured in some way.

This last point, stating constructs and relationship in ways they can be measured, is very important. For example, assume that a teacher is interested in knowing the degree to which the use of cooperative learning strategies within the classroom is effective. The first point that needs to be addressed is what is meant by *effective?* Effective at what—or in

Table 2.1   Moving from Observation to Researchable Question

Observation	Researchable Question
1. I have twenty students in my class.	How effective is a 1:20 ratio of teacher to students in promoting academic achievement?
2. As a result of our school moving toward full inclusion, I have children with physical disabilities within my class.	Would openly discussing the child's disability with the class help to have the child assimilated within the class?
3. Students seem to be having trouble taking complete and accurate class notes.	_____ _____ (To be completed by the reader)

what way? To be researchable, the concept of effectiveness needs to be more clearly and concisely defined. Transforming that initial curiosity into a testable question, the teacher may begin to ask if there is a relationship between the use of a cooperative learning activity and student achievement.

Table 2.1 provides some illustrations of teacher observations, which are reformulated as researchable questions and provide the reader with the opportunity to translate an observation into a researchable question.

◆ Reviewing the Literature

For the teacher acting as action researcher, a literature review provides a guide to defining the problem; selecting valid data-gathering devices; creating useful, valid **designs**; and recommending program interventions. Further, a review of the previous research can assist the teacher in anticipating possible difficulties that may be encountered.

A number of resources are available and can facilitate the search of the literature. Some of the basic sources are:

1. Resources in Education

2. Psychological Abstracts

3. Social Science Citation Index

4. The Education Index

5. Education Resources Information Centers (ERIC)

6. PsychINFO

In addition, many libraries now provide easy access to those and other literature databases via computer connections or CD-ROM.

◆ Stating the Hypothesis

What begins as a simple question about the relationships between several variables or constructs may develop into a sense of the expected answer or a prediction about the expected relationships. In this way, research questions take the shape of a research **hypothesis**, which is a more specific and predictive statement. For example, a teacher observing that students seem to have difficulty taking complete, accurate classroom notes may begin to wonder if there is any value in providing the students with a concept map at the beginning of a lecture. After reviewing pertinent literature, the teacher may feel that providing students with a concept map before a lecture will increase their ability to take complete, organized lecture notes. Through this process, the teacher has moved from making a simple observation, through the development of creating a researchable question, and ended with positing a testable hypothesis.

The research hypothesis, therefore, is an affirmative statement that predicts a research outcome or possible explanation of a relationship between two or more variables. Table 2.2 provides examples of how researchable questions may be transformed into testable hypotheses.

Table 2.2   Moving from Question to Hypothesis

Researchable Question	Testable Hypothesis
How effective is a 1:20 ratio of teacher to student?	Students in classes where there is a 1:20 teacher-to-student ratio will have higher academic achievement than those in a class with a 1:30 teacher-to-student ratio.
Would openly discussing the child's disability with the class help to have the child assimilated within the class?	Having the children ask Alfred questions about his braces and wheelchair will help them to develop a more positive attitude toward Alfred and facilitate his acceptance by his classmates.
Would providing a shy student with some type of classroom job help increase his interaction with other students?	_____ _____ _____
	(To be completed by the reader)

INCREASING THE VALIDITY OF THE CONCLUSIONS

The focus of action research is on the improvement of teaching and teacher decision making. For an action researcher, the goal of research is not just intellectual curiosity or a mere exercise in testing a hypothesis, but rather, the focus and purpose of the action research is to apply findings in a way that enhances practice decisions and positively impacts students and student achievement. In order for action research to be of use, it must produce results and conclusions that are valid and useful.

To conclude that the results observed were in fact due to the explanation provided, the researcher must be relatively certain that there is no other plausible explanation for the observed outcome. The validity of the conclusions increases when alternative explanations can be eliminated. For example, consider the teacher who decided to provide students with concept maps at the beginning of each class lecture and then observed an increase in the degree of accuracy and completeness of the students' notes. This teacher would be less assured of her conclusion that the improved note taking was a result of her implementation of concept maps if at the same time that she introduced concept maps she also shifted to the use of overhead (versus blackboard) notes. In this situation, the introduction of overheads provides a reasonable alternative explanation for the improved student note taking and therefore threatens the degree to which she can feel sure of her conclusions.

When a study has eliminated contaminants, or alternative explanations, it is said to have **internal validity.** Internal validity refers to the degree to which the relationship observed between two or more variables is meaningful in its own right and not due to something else. If there are alternative or rival explanations for the outcomes of the study, these alternatives are referred to as *threats* to the study's internal validity. As long as those threats remain, and other factors can possibly influence the outcome of the study, the researcher cannot be sure of the cause of the observations. Although it is obvious that action researchers should separate and eliminate contaminants from points of investigation, the question becomes "How?" This issue is addressed through the development of systematic, controlled methods of study (a point to be discussed in the remainder of the text).

♦ Developing and Implementing a Design

The goal of research is to establish a credible knowledge base. One approach to increasing the credibility of observations is to employ systematic, controlled methods of study. According to Fraenkel and Wallen (1993), a researcher can increase research rigor by

Action Research

Meeting the Needs of High-Ability Students

The process of moving from reflective teacher to action researcher is clearly articulated in Lynn Hughes's (1999) article: "Action Research and Practical Inquiry: How can I meet the needs of the high-ability student within my regular education classroom?"

Defining the Problem

Ms. Hughes felt that she was not meeting the needs of her high-ability students as a consequence of her school moving from a system of pull-out services for special education students to one in which all educational needs were met within the regular classroom.

Reviewing the Literature

The teacher began her research by reviewing the literature on the issue of gifted students in regular education classrooms. Some of the research she reviewed questioned the value of pull-out services for gifted students and other research highlighted the role regular education classrooms could play. Her reading indicated that regardless of the location, it was the quality of instruction that was most important in meeting the needs of the gifted students (p. 283). In addition to reviewing the literature, Ms. Hughes also checked with colleagues from her school and neighboring schools to gain their perspective and suggestions.

Developing a Hypothesis

As a result of the information she collected through reading and discussion, Ms. Hughes concluded that high-level learners needed to be challenged consistently. More specifically, she targeted three hypotheses to test (p. 286):

1. In-class enrichment activities will meet the needs of (her) high-ability learners.
2. In-class flexible groups will meet the needs of (her) high-ability learners.
3. Differentiated instruction will meet the needs of (her) high-ability learners.

Developing and Implementing a Design

Ms. Hughes decided to incorporate each of the following teaching strategies as part of her classroom regimen: enrichment and acceleration opportunities, flexible grouping, and differentiated instruction. She then assessed the effectiveness of each strategy for her high-ability students using various data-collection techniques.

Collecting and Analyzing Data

Ms. Hughes collected data through use of student questionnaires, parent interviews, classroom observations (by colleagues), and teacher–student portfolio conferences. The data collected were reviewed and sorted along general themes.

These data suggested that the following instruction strategies appeared to meet the needs of her high-ability students (p. 288):

1. Provide differentiated instruction and assessment.
2. Engage the students in academic decision making.
3. Use flexible groupings.
4. Plan for the right amount of enrichment versus acceleration for each individual child.

Application of Findings

Through the use of an action research approach to teaching, Ms. Hughes learned that she can meet the needs of not only the high-ability students but also the other students in her classroom. Further, her experience with this action research project resulted in the stimulation of many new questions to be answered about how to continue to improve her teaching effectiveness. As she noted: "I find each question answered brings yet another question in my quest to provide my high-ability students with the most effective educational experience" (p. 296). In this way, the reflective-teaching, action research cycle continues.

---

1. Employing standard procedures and conditions within the study. (See Chapter 5)

2. Collecting extensive information on the relevant characteristics of the subjects in the study. (See Chapter 3)

3. Keeping detailed information on the where, when, and what of the study. (See Chapter 4)

4. Implementing a proper design! (See Chapters 6–9)

◆ Data Collection and Analysis

The teacher, as action researcher, is interested in improving his or her teaching. To determine if the decisions made have had the desired effect, a teacher gathers and analyzes data. These data provide evidence of the effectiveness of the practice strategy. The information gathered by the teacher as action researcher can take many forms—test scores, frequencies of behaviors, student self-reports, and various documents and artifacts. Traditionally, these data sources have been categorized as either quantitative, which typically concerns number and frequencies, or qualitative procedures, which tend to address more descriptive, personal characteristics of the event (Kincheloe, 1991). A teacher as action researcher may gather data about the students' feelings and attitudes about learning or their creativity (**qualitative data**) in addition to test scores (**quantitative data**). The issues of qualitative and quantitative data will be explored further in upcoming chapters.

COOPERATIVE LEARNING EXERCISE

From Observation to Hypothesis

Below you will find a brief listing of areas of "observation" that a classroom teacher might make. Working with your classmates or colleagues:

1. Transform each observation into a researchable question.

2. Find one article or section of a textbook that provides insight into this situation and provides suggestions about what may be done to improve practice.

3. Select a specific action that may positively impact this situation and develop a testable hypothesis. When identifying expected outcomes, be sure to employ concrete, measurable definitions of the outcomes you seek.

Observation	Researchable Question	Testable Hypothesis
This teacher structures her class with lectures, small group exercises, and large group discussions.		
The class has two children who require the use of a wheelchair.		
This teacher allows her students to move about the class whenever they feel the need to stretch.		

Connections

The chapter closed with a case illustrating a teacher's attempt to systematically investigate the effectiveness of her teaching strategies. How unusual is this practice among teachers? Do other teachers attempt to reflect on their teaching decisions? Do teachers employ systematic observations and data collection in an attempt to assess their own effectiveness within the classroom? Let's find out.

Web site: Go to Classroom Connect at http://www.connectedteacher.com/home.asp

Go to Message Board. Post a message on the message board and share the feedback you receive with your colleagues or classmates.

SUGGESTED TOPICS
◆ What is your experience with employing reflective teaching and action research within your classroom?

◆ Do you employ techniques aimed at evaluating the impact of your teaching strategies? If so, would you explain?

INDIVIDUAL GUIDED PRACTICE EXERCISE

Action Research—with Me as Subject

The following exercise is provided to help you personalize the information presented in the chapter. Below is a list of experiences commonly encountered by teachers. Select one area of interest and develop an action research plan incorporating the fundamentals of research discussed in this chapter.

1. Areas of experience

   a. School projects

   b. Preparing for a test

   c. Making a presentation to the class

   d. Copying notes following a class lecture

2. Developing an action research plan

   a. Defining the problem

   b. Reviewing the literature

   c. Stating the hypothesis

   d. Developing and implementing a design

   e. Collecting and analyzing data

◆ Key Terms

descriptive question	hypothesis	quantitative data
design	internal validity	relationship question
difference question	qualitative data	researchable question

◆ Suggested Readings

Brause, R. S., & Mayher, J. S. (1991). *Search and research: What the inquiring teacher needs to know.* London: Falmer Press.

Fraenkel, J. R., & Wallen, N. E. (1993). *How to design and evaluate research in education* (2nd ed.). New York: McGraw-Hill.

Patton, M. Q. (1990). *Qualitative evaluation and research methods.* Newbury Park, CA: Sage.

◆ References

Berliner, C. D. (1987). Ways of thinking about students and classrooms by more and less experienced teachers. In J. Calderhead (Ed.), *Exploring teachers' thinking.* London: Cassell Educational Limited.

————. (1988). *The development of expertise in pedagogy.* Charles W. Hunt Memorial Lecture presented at annual meeting of the American Association of Colleges for Teacher Education (New Orleans).

Bogdan, R. C., & Biklen, S. K. (1998). *Qualitative research in education: An introduction to theory and methods.* Boston: Allyn & Bacon.

Drew, C. F. (1980). *Introduction to designing and conducting research* (2nd ed.). St. Louis, MO: C. V. Mosby.

Fraenkel, J. R., & Wallen, N. E. (1993). *How to design and evaluate research in education* (2nd ed.). New York: McGraw-Hill.

Hughes, L. (1999). Action research and practical inquiry: How can I meet the needs of the high ability student within my regular education classroom? *Journal of Education of the Gifted, 22*(3), 282–297.

Kagan, J. (1964). Impulsive and reflective children. In J. Krumbolz (Ed.), *Learning and the educational process.* Chicago: Rand McNally.

Kerlinger, F. N. (1986). *Foundations of behavioral research* (3rd ed.). New York: Holt, Rinehart & Winston.

Kincheloe, J. L. (1991). *Teachers as researchers: Qualitative inquiry as a path to empowerment.* London: Falmer Press.

INCREASING TEACHER EFFECTIVENESS: WORKING WITH THE UNIQUENESS OF "WHO" WE TEACH

Systematic Observation: A Research Skill Applied to the Understanding of Students' Cognitive Development

So the teacher goes up to a student and asks, "What is the sum of a positive 1 and a negative 1?" The student looks dumbfounded. However, the teacher says to the student, "Just fill the hole!" He keeps saying, "You can do it. Fill the hole." And all of a sudden the student appears reflective and then responds, "Zero!"

The scenario described by this teacher is from a scene in the movie *Stand and Deliver* (1988), in which the teacher, Jaime Escalante, attempts to teach the concept of negative and positive numbers. In the movie, Mr. Escalante employed the image of digging a hole in the sand at the beach, where the hole represented negative numbers and the mound of sand represented positive numbers. Encouraging the student to "fill the hole" served as an aid, a scaffold, to solving the problem.

What is equally impressive with this opening scenario is that the teacher watching the movie has drawn a number of subtle conclusions while "observing" the interaction between Mr. Escalante and the student. The movie watcher concludes that the student in the film was operating within the zone of proximal development (Vygotsky, 1993) and that because Mr. Escalante provided "scaffolding," or support, for the student's learning, the student was able to move to a position of solving the problem. This is an example of Vygotsky in action, as well as an example of the power of good observation and teacher reflection!

To be effective, a teacher needs to consider "who" they are teaching, as they plan the "what" and "how" (Parsons, Hinson, & Brown, 2001). As was evident in the movie scene, as well as the reaction of the teacher-observer, an important aspect of knowing students is understanding the nature of their cognitive development and the implications of a student's level of cognitive development on the development of a specific lesson plan. In order to be successful at meeting students' unique needs, teachers must be knowledgeable about developmental research and theory and also be skilled in making clear, insightful, valid observations about their students' behavior.

This chapter highlights the importance of developing skills in systematic observation as essential to acquiring a fuller understanding of students' unique capabilities. The chapter also discusses the importance of using these observational skills to assess the unique cognitive characteristics of students and to adjust teaching strategies in response to these observations.

◆ Chapter Objectives

Systematic observation is central to the process of research and effective teaching. As noted previously, the value of reflections is increased when they are based on data collected by way of systematic observation. This chapter highlights the "why" and "how" of systematic observation as applied to understanding students' level of cognitive development.

After reading this chapter, you should be able to do the following:

1 Explain the value of systematic observation to the classroom teacher.

2 Discuss the importance of developing systematic observations to the research process.

3 Explain what is meant by "operationalizing" a construct.

4 Formulate an observation into a researchable question and that question into a testable hypothesis.

5 Provide examples of student behavior reflecting the Piagetian concepts of assimilation, accommodation, and cognitive disequilibrium.

6 Provide examples of student behavior reflecting Vygotsky's concepts of zone of proximal development.

LEARNING TO OBSERVE: THE VALUE OF SYSTEMATIC OBSERVATION

For teachers to be effective, they must be effective observers, as well as be able to reflect, inquire, and critique their own interactions (Brandt, 1988). This ability to observe, interpret, and employ data in order to make instructional and classroom management decisions is a characteristic of "expert" teachers (Berliner, 1987, 1988; Borko & Shavelson, 1990; Carter et al., 1987; Leinhardt & Greeno, 1986; Peterson & Comeaux, 1987).

It may seem strange to think that educators who are in the beginning stages of incorporating action research into their teaching are told that as a first step they must develop skills in the area of observation. After all, teachers watch students all day. However, there is an important difference between *watching* and *observing*. A teacher may watch a student play by herself day after day during recess, and watch as the child is selected last by her classmates time after time when picking partners for group projects. An "observer" will begin to define the area of concern in clear, measurable, specific terms by asking questions such as: "Is the stu-

CONTENT MAP 3

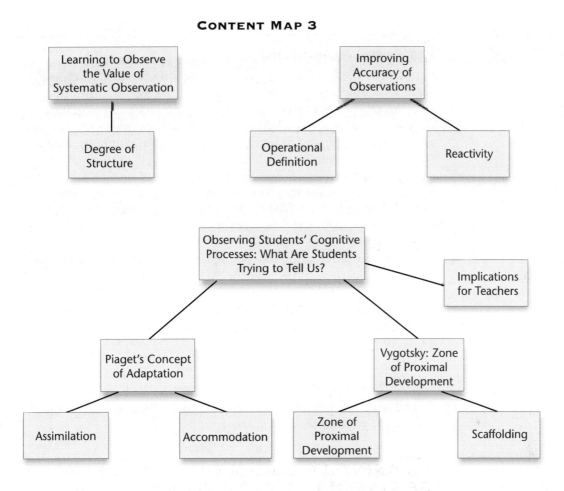

dent actively rejected or is she simply consistently overlooked by her peers?" "Is there a specific area of skill deficit interfering with her peer interactions?" "Does she have the skills necessary to allow her to enter into a group?" "Does she seem to understand the dynamics of group membership?" Obviously, the answers to those and many other questions will determine what intervention strategies the teacher employs and how the teacher defines and measures "success" with this child. The skill of observation lays the groundwork for identifying the area of concern, implementing an intervention, evaluating the effectiveness of the intervention, and maintaining and generalizing the effects of the intervention.

◆ Observations: Degree of Structure

Observations can be more or less structured. A **structured observation** is best used when specific behaviors are targeted in advance and lend themselves to being assessed in terms of frequency, duration, or magnitude. A *frequency count* allows the researcher to know how often a particular behavior occurs during a specified time period (e.g., how many times a student blurts out an answer during science class), whereas a *duration measure* looks for the length of time the behavior continues (e.g., the amount of time a student remains off task), and *magnitude* records the behavior's intensity. Using categories of frequency, duration, and magnitude, the action researcher can employ quantitative analysis. For example, a teacher who is interested in seeing the effects of a classroom management strategy on reducing a student's disruptive behavior may keep a tally of the frequency of "calling-out" behavior, both before and after the introduction of the classroom management strategy, as a way of monitoring intervention effectiveness.

Unstructured observations are best employed when the researcher is not exactly clear about the behaviors to be observed or intends to gain a more global picture of the situation. The researcher records his or her observations in field notes that provide a contemporary record of the important elements observed. These field notes should be recorded as soon as possible after observing the behavior and may include descriptions of

1. People: individuals, groups, subgroups, roles, and positions
2. Places: location of activities and events, physical arrangement, and layout of the setting
3. Activities: particular actions and related actions
4. Objects: materials, equipment, furnishings
5. Purposes: goals of activities observed
6. Time: sequencing and timing of events (including frequency and duration)
7. Feelings: emotional responses exhibited.

This type of approach is often used by those studying others in different cultures, or when the behavior under investigation cannot be easily categorized. Teachers may use unstructured observations to assess children at play in the recess yard, or to record the interactions of students in a work group.

The use of behavioral observation often requires some specific training on the part of the observer. For those using unstructured observation, training can assist in developing the skills needed to process the massive amount of data observed. For researchers employing structured observations, training can help them stay true to the original categories by allowing them to correctly discern what fits into each category and what does not.

◆ Improving Accuracy of Observations

The goal of action research is to improve practice through the use of applied research. This goal will be impossible to accomplish if the behavior of concern, the intervention employed, and the results of the intervention are not accurately and objectively identified and defined. For this reason, the need for clear and concrete definitions and systematic observations is a pragmatic concern for the action researcher.

In order to have a testable hypothesis, the factors under study (i.e., the problem, the intervention, and the outcome) must be identified in clear, unambiguous, measurable terms. Defining terms in a concrete manner allows for the gathering of data and ultimately for making determinations regarding intervention efficacy. Although many variables of interest to the action researcher, such as achievement, aggression, and discipline, are defined in the dictionary, knowing the definition of those constructs does not automatically allow for direct observation. As defined in the dictionary or through common usage, those constructs cannot be measured directly. Because terms can be vague, subjective, and open to many different interpretations, they must be defined in a more objective and precise manner. The action researcher increases **objectivity** and precision by operationally defining the terms relevant to the research question.

◆ Operational Definitions

With apologies to the makers of the movie *Forrest Gump,* operationalizing a construct is simply stating that "a construct is as a construct does." Therefore, the teacher attempting to "operationally" define the variables under consideration specifies the activities or operations used to measure those variables. The score or the findings from this measurement will serve as the **operational definition** of the concept.

Consider the example of Mr. McKee, a seventh-grade social studies teacher, who is frustrated because his attempts to integrate cooperative learning activities throughout his curriculum "just aren't working" in most of his classes. According to Mr. McKee, when trying to make the groups "work better," he has "tried a lot of things" and has noticed that some classes "do better for a while," but that some of his sections just never "seem to click with group work." Obviously, Mr. McKee's first challenge is to define what he means by "just aren't working." What is it that he is observing that leads him to conclude that his learning activities "just aren't working"? He may simply mean that in some of his classes, assignments are not completed on time to a satisfactory level of proficiency. If the groups were formed to enhance cooperation and cohesion among his students, the teacher's concern may also revolve around the internal dynamics of the group. A third possibility is that

Table 3.1   Operationalizing Constructs

Variable/Construct of Interest	Suggested Ways to Operationalize
Academic Achievement	1. Standardized Achievement Tests
	2. Teacher-Made Test
	3. (Reader completes) _____
Student Enjoyment	1. Student Self-Reported Survey
	2. The Frequency of Student Laughter
	3. (Reader completes) _____
Student Cooperation	1. Frequency of "Sharing" Behaviors
	2. (Reader completes) _____
	3. (Reader completes) _____

structuring and monitoring these group activities are demanding more of his time and energy than he feels appropriate, not allowing him to cover the required curriculum. Obviously, in this example, defining the problem as the teacher is experiencing it determines what questions will follow, what data will be collected, what interventions will be implemented, and how success of those interventions will be defined. Clear, specific, objective language is the first step in defining the problem operationally and in directing our observations.

Table 3.1 provides a number of examples of ways to operationalize specific constructs and also provides the reader with an opportunity to operationalize others.

◆ Reactivity

In addition to having clearly identified and operationally defined variables, action researchers interested in improving the accuracy and validity of their observations must take steps to reduce the possibility of reactivity. **Reactivity** refers to the possibility that the very act of observing influences what is being observed. Consider the elevated dramatics often exhibited by adolescents once they are aware they are being observed. Obviously, if the goal is to observe the student performing in the "purest" form, uninfluenced by artificial factors such as impressing the observer, then the influence of being observed must be reduced.

Although addressing issues of reactivity presents a unique problem for the action researcher who uses observational techniques of data gathering, the occurrence of reactivity can be reduced by using less direct methods, such as one-way mirrors. Reactivity can also be reduced when both the observer and the method of recording are part of the "natural" experience of the participants within that environment. Allowing time for the observer to become a participant in the setting can help reduce reactivity. Continued exposure often desensitizes participants to the fact that they are being observed. One of the benefits of the teacher serving as the researcher is that the teacher is already part of the natural environment. Case Illustration 3-1 demonstrates how a teacher, Miss Lammey, used an observational approach to data collection.

Case Illustration 3-1
Miss Lammey as Observer

Miss Lammey was interested in increasing the students' level of personal reflection and disclosure about assigned reading material. For that purpose, she employed small-group, cooperative-learning assignments in her classroom. In order to assess the impact of those cooperative-learning assignments, she sat in the small groups to observe their discussions. Initially, she observed the students attempting to put on their best performance after all she *was* the teacher! Once it became apparent that the students ignored her presence in the group, she began to record data that she felt gave evidence of personal reflection and disclosure. In her observations, she focused on two types of data. First, she recorded the frequency with which "I-statements" were made, evidencing self-disclosure. She also decided to record the duration of the discussion as it focused on the sharing of personal experiences.

An advantage of using observational recordings is that the researcher is not required to guess or infer what is going on. What is observed is recorded. A limitation, however, is that not all targets of research center around directly observable behaviors. For example, a student's attitude about a particular class or teaching strategy doesn't lend itself to direct observation. Therefore, action researchers often blend the use of observation techniques and the collection of quantitative data (e.g., frequency counts of behavior) with more qualitative methods of research. For example, in addition to recording the frequency of a specific behavior, the action researcher may take detailed notations about behaviors and events and the contexts surrounding those events and behaviors. This issue of employing qualitative methods of data collection is explored in greater depth in Chapter 4.

In order to demonstrate the application of systematic observation in service of educational research and practice, we will briefly discuss the works of Jean Piaget and Lev Vygotsky. The intent is to illustrate a component of educational research, rather than fully explain the cognitive theories of those two developmental theorists. Readers interested in a more elaborate explanation of those cognitive developmental theories are referred to primary references listed in the reference section of this chapter.

OBSERVING STUDENTS' COGNITIVE PROCESSES

What are the students trying to tell us?

One theorist who was quite skilled in employing systematic observation for analyzing children's cognitive processes was Swiss psychologist Jean Piaget. Piaget used observation and a clinical-descriptive method to collect data that supported his theory on how humans gather and organize information. Piaget asked children carefully selected questions and recorded their responses. He also gathered data by way of meticulous observations of children's behavior. Although he frequently observed small numbers of children, his observations were longitudinal in nature; that is, he followed the development of these same children over a period of years. Although a large part of his later work was based on the testing of more than 1,500 subjects (Inhelder & Piaget, 1958) and statistical analysis of his findings (Piaget, 1964; Piaget, 1969), it started with the systematic observations of his own three children.

◆ Piaget's Concept of Adaptation

The cornerstone of Piaget's theory is the concept of adaptation, or the way we attempt to adjust to the various demands of our environment. Piaget believed that humans begin this adaptation process by developing **schemata**, or mental structures, which allow us to identify and begin to "understand" experiences. According to Piaget, as new experiences in life are encountered, we attempt to cognitively adapt to those new experiences by making meaning of them. Two processes, assimilation and accommodation, are used in this adaptation.

◆ Assimilation and Accommodation

The first strategy for adapting to a new experience is to make meaning by using a currently existing schema or way of cognitively organizing information. This is a process Piaget termed **assimilation.** For example, perhaps you have observed a toddler who, in the process of developing language, begins to call a dog a "bow-wow." If, when encountering a small sheep, this toddler exclaims, "bow-wow," the process of assimilation is being demonstrated. The toddler in this illustration attempts to make sense of the new experience (i.e., the sheep) using an old schema (i.e., four legs, small, furry, etc. = bow-wow).

Sometimes, however, new experiences simply do not fit into old schemata. For example, consider the surprise an infant may display as a result of first developing the schema that small, handheld items are fun to bang. When given a rattle, small ball, or even a bottle cap, the child may begin to bang the item on the table, apparently enjoying the noise it makes. However, what happens when the child gets hold of a fresh egg? Initially, the child will attempt to assimilate this new item, using the previous "banging schema." This time, however, rather than hearing the enjoyable banging sound, the child experiences the ooze of a cracked egg. The look on the child's face will illustrate the impact of being unable to assimilate a new experience. The child may be so distressed that he begins to cry. But watch! When given a new item, he may now be more cautious and may test its "bang-ability." Through the process of **accommodation**, the child has developed new cognitive structures and expanded his ability to cognitively adapt to life's experiences. The child may first lightly tap the item, observe, and then more vigorously tap the item. Why the caution?

The child now experiments with items before banging them because he now has two schemata to use while making sense of handheld items. One schema is that some handheld items can be banged and they make noise; the second schema is that some items can be banged and they break!

◆ Vygotsky: An Alternative to Piaget

An alternative to Piaget's approach was offered by the Russian psychologist, Lev Semonovich Vygotsky. Vygotsky, who died more than 50 years ago at the age of 38, developed ideas about the influence of culture and language on cognitive development. Recent translations of his work demonstrate that he provides a viable option to many of Piaget's ideas (Vygotsky, 1978; Vygotsky, 1993). Two of the constructs pivotal to Vygotsky's view of cognitive development and learning are the zone of proximal development and scaffolding.

◆ The Zone of Proximal Development

Vygotsky believed that when children function and solve problems independently they are working within the **zone of actual development.** However, he believed that there are times when a child can solve problems only with support, and this he identified as the **zone of proximal development.** He posited that learning takes place when the child is working within the zone of proximal development, that is, when a child is presented with tasks that she is not yet capable of doing herself but can successfully accomplish if given assistance by a peer or teacher.

Consider the situation in which a child is at the board attempting to complete an algebra problem, solving for an unknown. As others at the board finish their problems and begin returning to their seats, the teacher notes that this remaining student is starting to show signs of frustration. Although it is clear that the student has been unable to successfully solve the problem on his own (zone of actual development), it is not clear if the problem is simply beyond his ability or within his zone of proximal development.

In order to assess if the problem lies within the child's zone of proximal development, the teacher approaches the board and whispers, "Remember, whatever you do to one side of the equation you need to do to the other." The teacher steps back and watches as the student looks at the problem, returns to his solution, begins to correct it, and finally arrives at the correct answer. Clearly, this was a situation in which the child could solve a problem with support or mediation.

◆ Scaffolding

The previous example illustrates a student operating within the zone of proximal development and shows the value of teacher observation and intervention in facilitating learning. Observing the student's level of frustration as evidence that the student was not in the zone of actual development, the teacher approached with the intent to intervene. Observing that the student was close to the solution (i.e., proximal), the teacher assumed that with a little mediation, or assistance, the student would be able to grasp the solution. In this way, the teacher provided **scaffolding** by way of the reminder in order to assist the student in constructing an answer to the problem.

For Vygotsky, social interaction is more than simply a method of teaching. It is the base for higher mental processes such as problem solving. The teacher in this case provided a clue (a reminder) that served as a support (a scaffold) for the student to build a firm understanding of the problem-solving process. The result is a student successfully resolving the problem at hand.

◆ Implications for Teachers?

There are a number of implications to be derived from the theories of Piaget and Vygotsky. However, the value of these theories and their implications for the classroom teacher, in any one classroom, needs to be "tested" by the teacher turned action researcher.

◆ From Piaget

First, when presenting new information and challenging experiences to students, teachers should expect a degree of resistance. Why? Because new experiences require adaptation, which is not always easy. Second, because the first attempt to cognitively adapt involves assimilation (or understanding from within a currently existing framework), any new material that can be tied to existing schemata may be more easily processed and stored than material that is novel and requires the development of new schemata. Therefore, tying new learning to previous learning may be a useful tool in helping students process new information.

However, this same tendency to assimilate experiences can lead to some confusion and mistakes when the new experience is actually different than that previously encountered. Consider the situation in which a student's only experience with the word "Indian" is through old television presentations of cowboy and Indian movies. The student may initially have difficulty "conceptualizing" Native Americans as different from the stereotypes depicted on television. Or this same student may assume that an East Indian would wear feather headpieces or live in tepees.

For this reason, when teaching a new lesson, it may prove helpful to have students discuss what they think is meant by the various terms about to be discussed. In this way, a teacher helps the students relate new information to something they already know (assimilate) while highlighting differences in order to modify pre-existing beliefs and build new schemata (accommodate).

Consider the movie scene described in the beginning the chapter. The teacher portrayed in the movie used the images of a hole in the sand and a mound of sand to help students "assimilate" the new concepts of positive and negative numbers. However, later in the scene, the teacher uses the students' inability to assimilate in order to increase student interest and motivation to attend class. Before the class period ends, the teacher has the students recite: "A negative times a negative is a positive." He has them repeat this over and over. As the bell rings, signifying the end of the class, he asks: "Why?" The question has no immediate answer. The students searching their schemata have nothing they can call forth to make sense of the question. As a result, they are placed in a state of **cognitive disequilibrium**, a state of tension that they need to alleviate. This tension will be reduced in the next class, when the teacher explains the answer to his question, and the students are able to develop a new schema for answering those types of questions.

This teacher not only knows the benefits of using Piagetian concepts in his teaching decisions, but is also an excellent observer of his students' responses. He recognizes when they are assimilating, when they are accommodating, and when they are in stages of cognitive disequilibrium, and he uses this information to give shape to his teaching decisions.

◆ From Vygotsky

Following upon Vygotsky's theory, it appears that teachers should identify a student's zone of proximal development and develop instructional plans that not only target that area, but also incorporate appropriate social interaction and scaffolding to assist the child working in this zone. However, to do this effectively, a teacher must employ observational skills to discern when a child is in the zone of proximal development and when specific scaffolds, such as hints, aids, or reminders, are or are not effective. Being observant and using recording techniques to note observations of a child's ability prior to and following the application of scaffolds can become part of a dynamic assessment technique used to test both the upper and lower levels of the child's zone of proximal development. The teacher can also use these notations to develop an instructional plan, which includes graduated teacher interventions (scaffolds) at different levels of task complexity (Greenfield, 1984).

COOPERATIVE LEARNING EXERCISE

Observing Zones of Proximal Development

Directions

Working in teams of two, select a particular child that you could "shadow" or follow through a portion of a school day. The child could be in preschool, kindergarten, elementary, or high school. Observe this child in a specific class period (e.g., mathematics, social studies, reading, etc.) or through a specific classroom activity (e.g., working with letters and letter recognition, solving math problems, working at a science lab table, etc.).

1. Identify tasks that appeared too easy for that child. Describe what you were observing that led to this conclusion.

2. Identify tasks that appeared too hard for that child. Describe what you were observing that led to this conclusion.

3. Describe an incident when the child was apparently working within his or her zone of proximal development. What did you observe that suggested that this was the child's zone of proximal development? What scaffolding was used by the teacher? How

Action Research

The Value of Peer Interaction for Cognitive Development

Joan Mullin, a third-grade teacher at Columbus Public Schools, described an action research project (Hildebrand, Ludeman, & Mullin, 1999), which provided additional support for Piaget's belief in the value of peer interaction in facilitating development (Piaget, 1967) and Vygotsky's view of the role that interaction among peers plays in the transmission of knowledge (Vygotsky, 1962).

Method
Ms. Mullin attempted to build on the positive experience her students had with conference-based language arts instruction by having the students write and solve original mathematics word problems. The students challenged their peers by using an activity called the Mathematician's Chair. In this activity, one student would share her word problem with peers, who in turn attempted to solve it. In addition, peers provided constructive feedback to the child who created the problem.

Prior to initiating the teaching strategy, the teacher had the students write word problems as a pretest procedure. Post-test data were collected later in the year, after the students had been involved with the Mathematician's Chair strategy.

Data Collection and Analysis
Ms. Mullin developed a rubric to evaluate students' performance in writing mathematics word problems. Scoring was accomplished by assigning a point value based on (1) clarity of the mathematical statements, (2) their solvability, (3) the structure and creativity of the problems, and (4) the language used in the mathematical statements.

Postproblem
The teacher charted the results of the pre- and post-problem writing scores. These data demonstrated an improvement in the students' writing and ability to solve original mathematics word problems. The teacher also used a student attitude questionnaire in a pretest and post-test procedure, which indicated that the students not only improved in skills development, but also improved in the way they perceived themselves as mathematics problem solvers.

Conclusions
Although the intent of this action research project was to improve teaching effectiveness, its use of systematic observation and data collection also provided support for Piaget's and Vygotsky's belief that a child benefits from interaction with knowledgeable peers. Through interaction, critical feedback, and challenging questioning of peers, Ms. Mullin's students improved their ability to write and solve original mathematics word problems. Further, she found that the more knowledgeable peers benefited from the process of "making [their] ideas more explicit, thereby rendering what is known more clear and objective" (p. 441).

effective was the scaffolding? What did you observe that led to your conclusions regarding effectiveness?

4. Reflect on your observations and the process of systematic observation. What difficulty did you experience in making your observations? Did your observations differ from those of your partner? If so, why? What could you have done to increase the effectiveness and consistency of your team's observations? (Hint: Did you clearly define what you were looking for?)

Connections

Observations on Students' Cognitive Processing

The purpose of this exercise is to provide the opportunity to dialogue with professionals who observe students' cognitive processing and adapt their teaching strategies to facilitate learning and cognitive development.

DIRECTIONS

◆ Go to: http://www.teachers.net

◆ Go to the "Chatboard" and post a message, such as one of the following:

1. "How do you determine when a child is simply unable to understand and complete a learning exercise, or when the child is in the zone of proximal development and in need of scaffolding?"

2. "Could you provide a real-life example of your use of scaffolding to promote student learning and explain what you 'look for' to know that the scaffolding was effective?"

3. "Would you share an example of an activity that you use or have used to stimulate cognitive disequilibrium as a means of increasing student interest and motivation and describe what you look for to know that the activity was effective?"

◆ Share and discuss your findings with your classmates or colleagues.

INDIVIDUAL GUIDED PRACTICE EXERCISE

Looking for Cognitive Disequilibrium

Cognitive development occurs in response to the experience of cognitive disequilibrium. When students are presented with a new experience, they encounter the tension of cognitive disequilibrium, which serves as a motivator energizing them to make meaning of this new experience. In this way, children are open to new learning events. Therefore, a useful strategy for effective teaching would be to introduce new learning experiences by first creating cognitive disequilibrium.

The following exercise directs you to consider the value and impact of creating cognitive dissonance as an initial experience to a lesson:

1. Select a specific focus for your lesson plan (e.g., introducing the scientific method, teaching the causes for the Civil War, considering the concept of evolution, etc.).

2. Develop a lesson plan that begins with an exercise or an experience aimed at creating cognitive disequilibrium in your students.

For example, rather than jumping into a lecture or into work-sheets about the topic of the scientific method, perhaps you could pose a riddle that requires deductive reasoning or employ a demonstration such as using a mixture of chemicals that provides a surprise outcome and then ask the students to explain what has happened.

3. As the students begin to respond, observe the process of assimilation. Do they attempt to solve the riddle or explain the phenomenon based on previous schemata?

4. Observe the looks on the students' faces as they offer explanations based on old schemata that fail in this situation. How does this "cognitive disequilibrium" look to the observer?

5. Observe and describe the process through which the students begin to modify old schemata or develop new ones (i.e., accommodation). Do the students build on each other's ideas? Do they seem to spontaneously come to some creative insight? Do they need your hints, your support (Vygotsky's scaffolding)?

6. Finally, how would you assess the effectiveness of using an event that stimulates cognitive disequilibrium as a way of introducing a lesson?

◆ Key Terms

accommodation	objectivity	structured observation
adaptation	operational definition	systematic observation
assimilation	reactivity	unstructured observation
cognitive disequilibrium	scaffolding	zone of actual development
observations	schemata	zone of proximal development

◆ Suggested Readings

Adler, P. A., & Adler, P. (1994). Observational techniques. Pp. 377–392 in N. K. Denzin & Y. S. Lincoln (Eds.), *Handbook of qualitative research*. Thousand Oaks, CA: Sage.

Cowan, P. A. (1978). *Piaget with feeling*. New York: Holt, Rinehart & Winston.

Stake, R. E. (1994). Case studies. Pp. 236–246 in N. K. Denzin & Y. S. Lincoln (Eds.), *Handbook of qualitative research*. Thousand Oaks, CA: Sage.

◆ References

Berk, L. E., & Garvin, R. A. (1984). Development of private speech among low-income Appalachian children. *Developmental Psychology, 20,* 271–286.

Berliner, C. D. (1987). Ways of thinking about students and classrooms by more and less experienced teachers. In J. Calderhead (Ed.), *Exploring teachers' thinking.* London: Cassell Educational Limited.

—————. (1988). *The development of expertise in pedagogy.* Charles W. Hunt Memorial Lecture presented at annual meeting of the American Association of Colleges for Teacher Education (New Orleans).

Borko, H., & Shavelson, R. J. (1990). Teachers' decision making. In B. Jones & L. Idols (Eds.), *Dimensions of thinking and cognitive instruction.* Hillsdale, NJ: Erlbaum.

Brandt, R. (1988). *Content of the curriculum: ASCD Yearbook.* Alexandria, VA: ASCD.

Carter, K., Sabers, D., Cushing, K., Pinnegar, S., & Berliner, D. (1987). Processing and using information about students: A study of expert, novice and postulant teachers. *Teaching and Teacher Education, 3*(2), 147–157.

Greenfield, P. M. (1984). Theory of the teacher in learning activities. Pp. 117–138 in B. Rogoff & J. Lave (Eds.), *Everyday cognition: Its development in social context.* Cambridge, MA: Harvard University Press.

Hildebrand, C., Ludeman, C. J., & Mullin, J. (1999). Integrating mathematics with problem solving using the mathematician's chair. *Teaching Children Mathematics,* March, 434–441.

Inhelder, B., & Piaget, J. (1958). *The growth of logical thinking from childhood to adolescence.* New York: Basic Books.

Karpov, Y. V., & Bransford, J. D. (1995). Vygotsky and the doctrine of empirical and theoretical learning. *Educational Psychologist, 30,* 61–66.

Kozulin, A., & Presseisen, B. Z. (1995). Mediated learning experience and psychological tools: Vygotsky's and Feuerstein's perspectives in a study of student learning. *Educational Psychologist, 30,* 67–75.

Leinhardt, G., & Greeno, J. G. (1986). The cognitive skill of teaching. *Educational Leadership, 49*(1), 20–25.

Parsons, R. D., Hinson, S. L., & Sardo-Brown, D. (2001). *Educational psychology: A practitioner–researcher model of teaching.* Belmont, CA: Wadsworth.

Peterson, P. L., & Comeaux, M. A. (1987). Assessing the teacher as a reflective professional: New perspectives on teacher evaluation. Pp. 132–152 in A. Wolfolk (Ed.), *Research perspectives on the graduate preparation of teachers.* Englewood Cliffs, NJ: Prentice-Hall.

Piaget, J. (1964). Development and learning. In R. Ripple & V. Rockcastle (Eds.), *Piaget rediscovered.* Washington, DC: U.S. Office of Education, National Science Foundation.

—————. (1967). *Six psychological studies.* London: London University Press.

—————. (1969). *Science of education and the psychology of the child.* New York: Viking.

Stand and Deliver (1988). Warner Bros.

Vygotsky, L. S. (1962). *Thought and language.* New York: John Wiley & Sons.

—————. (1978). *Mind in society.* Cambridge, MA: Harvard University Press.

—————. (1993). *The collected works of L. S. Vygotsky,* vol. 2 (J. Knox and C. Stevens, Trans.). New York: Plenum.

CHAPTER 4

Qualitative and Quantitative Methodology: Tools for the Action Researcher

t's funny. I am familiar with Erikson's life stages and I understand that adolescents are working hard to develop their **identities.** To see how important it is for them to try on these various personalities, testing which one or which combination fits, is really wonderful. But I wonder if there is a way I could use that tendency to get them more fully involved in

their readings and classroom discussions. It
would be great if I could use this somehow
to raise their achievement levels!

The teacher depicted in our opening scenario is astute in her observations and is starting to ponder a very researchable question. Can a teacher use the adolescent's drive for ego identity as a teaching tool? This is one of many questions that may emerge when teachers as action researchers begin to consider how the psychosocial needs and characteristics of their students may affect academic performance and achievement. Further, it is through the systematic collection and interpretation of both **quantitative** and **qualitative data** that this teacher may find the answer to her question.

♦ Chapter Objectives

Observing our students and employing techniques to allow us to more fully understand their attitudes, values, and opinions of self and others provide us with the data needed to more fully understand the uniqueness of each student. These same data then serve as a foundation from which to increase the effectiveness of our teaching.

This chapter discusses the process of data collection, organization, and analysis for both qualitative and quantitative research. In addition, the chapter provides a brief discussion of Erik Erikson's stages of psychosocial development. The discussion of Erikson is brief and intended only as an illustration of the utility of qualitative and quantitative research in guiding teacher decisions regarding effective classroom practices. Readers interested in a more developed discussion of Erikson are referred to the readings listed at the end of this chapter.

After reading this chapter, you should be able to do the following:

1 Explain what is meant by *qualitative* and *quantitative research* and the characteristics associated with both types of research.

2 Identify the steps necessary for analyzing qualitative data.

3 Describe what is meant by *descriptive statistics*.

4 Define three forms of central tendency: mode, mean, and median.

5 Explain what is meant by *measure of dispersion*.

6 Describe how a qualitative approach can be used to analyze our students' **psychosocial crisis** (Erikson, 1950).

RESEARCH: A VALUABLE TOOL FOR THE CLASSROOM TEACHER

For teachers turned action researchers, the thought of engaging in complicated, abstract mathematical formulas and processes in order to validate their professional experience is often viewed as a waste of time and energy, or worse, as a traumatic encounter. And although many researchers employ complicated, abstract mathematical formulas and processes, this is only one form of research and may not be the method of choice for any one action researcher. Research can provide invaluable

CONTENT MAP 4

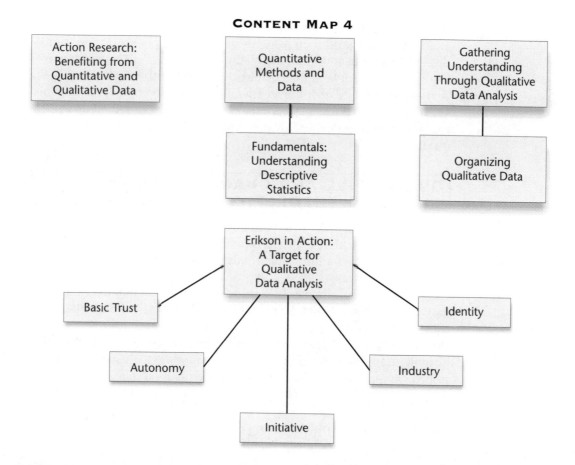

information for a teacher. But for research to be of value to the classroom teacher, the researcher must use a good and useful research design, for example, collecting quantitative information on specific factors or variables and emphasizing the quality and importance of (1) the relationship of all participants (teacher and students) involved and (2) the rich context and contextual value to understanding the information gathered.

QUALITATIVE AND QUANTITATIVE RESEARCH: SHARING A DYNAMIC PROCESS

In many ways, the process of conducting research is the same, whether from a qualitative or quantitative framework. Action research, be it quantitative or qualitative in nature, is basically a systematic process of collecting and analyzing data in order to acquire knowledge and improve practice. And, as discussed in Chapter 2, there are certain "basic" steps to be taken in any research, regardless if it is qualitative or quantitative in nature.

The action researcher using either model will need to engage in a dynamic process of identifying a problem; developing research questions or hypotheses; determining a design; collecting, analyzing, and interpreting data; and then using those data to guide practice decisions. However, the data collected, the methods of analysis, and the interpretations derived will be influenced by the nature of the design employed, be it quantitative or qualitative. Therefore, it is important for the action researcher to understand the uniqueness and value of each approach and, when appropriate, to integrate both forms of research to derive maximum benefit.

QUALITATIVE AND QUANTITATIVE RESEARCH: DIFFERING THEORETICAL FOUNDATIONS

What becomes apparent when initially comparing qualitative and quantitative research is that researchers typically collect different types of data for each. For example, quantitative studies often report on numerical data, such as mean scores and probability levels, when drawing conclusions about the variables being studied; whereas qualitative studies may provide rich context-driven narratives. But there are other, perhaps somewhat more subtle differences that exist. In quantitative research, the researchers go to great lengths to remove themselves as much as possible from the findings of the study, attempting to create a controlled environment in which to collect their data. Qualitative researchers, on the other hand, may find themselves to be active participants in the events they are studying. It is one thing, for example, to collect frequency recordings or test scores taken from controlled observations of a group of people within a laboratory setting (quantitative data and methods) and quite another to live among those people and, through the use of interviewing, collect their stories and folklore (qualitative data and methods).

Although these differences are important ones, it is overly simplistic to focus on them without understanding the more fundamental, theoretical differences that influence all aspects of the qualitative and quantitative study. Why is qualitative research more context dependent than quantitative research? And why are the researcher roles so different in the two types of studies? Those and other differences can be traced from the theoretical foundations of each model.

◆ Phenomenological Foundation of Qualitative Research

Qualitative research rests on a **phenomenological foundation** (Mason & Bramble, 1997) and as such, has a strong focus on deriving meaning of a phenomenon through understanding the context in which it occurs. Therefore, whereas quantitative researchers attempt to control or remove elements they consider "extraneous variables" from the context of a study (variables that may affect the phenomenon being studied, including the effect of the researcher), the qualitative researcher views the phenomenon under study as part of a whole, affected by and in turn affecting the environment in which the phenomenon occurs. Another characteristic of a phenomenological approach, which serves as the foundation for qualitative research, is the belief that there is no absolute truth, but rather multiple truths depending on one's perspective. As such, perspective, or how one understands and interprets events, becomes an important focus for this type of approach.

◆ Logical Positivism: Theoretical Foundation of Quantitative Research

In contrast, quantitative research has theoretical foundations in an orientation called **logical positivism** (Phillips, 1987). Logical positivism posits that only those things that can be observed and measured can be said to exist. From within this mode of inquiry, objectivity and quantification are emphasized. Further, the directive to gain objectivity forces the experimenter to control the observed events. While phenomenologists study an event holistically from within the naturally occurring context, positivists prefer to break the event down into small, measurable units and consider surrounding events occurring in the environment to be extraneous variables to be controlled or eliminated so that the event under study can be examined in isolation.

◆ Different—Yet Similarly Valuable

The differences in theoretical underpinnings help explain differences in quantitative and qualitative research methods, such as type of data collected (numbers and probability levels versus field observations and in-depth interviews), the nature of the data reported (descriptive and inferential statistics versus narrative, descriptive conclusions), the definition of a "valid" study (one that rules out alternative hypotheses and is generalizable beyond the sample versus the extent to which the explanations reflect the real world), and the role of the researcher.

Though differences in theoretical foundations (i.e., positivism versus phenomenology) and approaches (i.e., nature of the data collected, type of data analysis) exist between qualitative and quantitative research methods, it is inappropriate to assume that one research methodology is superior to the other, and therefore is the method of choice. Rather, the methodology should be determined by the nature of the research question. What type of research best fits the needs of the researcher? Further, as is evident throughout this text, we believe that the action researcher may find it helpful to incorporate both research methodologies, but to do so requires a fuller understanding of each.

QUANTITATIVE METHODS AND DATA

Quantitative research employs methods that attempt to categorize and assign numbers to an experience or event. The teacher, for example, interested in investigating a student's impulsive verbal responses in the classroom may use quantitative methods by recording a mark on a card each time the child calls out in class and counting the frequency of that behavior. The check marks can then be summed and used to reflect the degree of impulsive responding exhibited by the student during a specified observational period. These data can be compared with similar data collected at another point in time or for another student as a way of assessing the potential value of the teacher's intervention strategies.

Quantitative researchers are interested in collecting data that can be manipulated via statistical analysis. Thus, counting the frequency of a behavior or measuring the degree of a response or a score on a test provide a quantitative researcher with "data" that can be mathematically and statistically manipulated.

◆ Using Descriptive Statistics

Descriptive statistics are simple ways of calculating values that represent overall characteristics of a body of data, with the goal of describing a specific group of data with no concern for generalizing conclusions beyond those data. Descriptive statistics provide the action researcher with an economical tool for organizing and describing data.

◆ Measures of Central Tendency

One type of descriptive statistics, **measures of central tendency**, are frequently used by action researchers. For example, consider the teacher attempting to describe a student's test performance for a particular marking period. The teacher may choose to use the **mean** as the statistic that best describes the student's performance. The mean is an arithmetic average and, as a measure of central tendency, is computed by summing all of the individual scores and then dividing by the number of scores. In this case, the mean, or the student's test score average, is a score that represents the collection of all the data reflecting that student's performance on all the individual tests administered during the marking period. Each time the student takes a test, his score is recorded. The scores are then summed (i.e., added together) and divided by the number of tests administered during the marking period. Dividing the total number of points by the number of tests taken yields the average score (or the mean test score) for that student. In this case, one score, a mean, provides a description of an overall set of test performances for that student, and only that student.

Measures of central tendency are statistics that provide a reference point from which to understand an array of data. The mean takes into consideration each individual score as it contributes to a total, which then is divided by the number of scores. Educators often employ the mean as a way of describing a student's performance in the classroom. The student's grade point average is a mean. Because the mean reflects the contribution of each individual score, it is very sensitive to extreme scores. A single large number or score can elevate the mean to such a degree that it may no longer fairly represent the "average" level of performance. Similarly, an extremely low score will reduce the mean. This sensitivity to extreme scores may make the mean an inappropriate measure to use in a data analysis. Consider an extreme example: Assume a teacher monitors a student's inappropriate calling out in math class and records the following frequencies for a five-day time trial: 17, 18, 16, 17, 2. She then calculates the mean to be 14. The teacher must decide if the mean of 14 fairly represents the average amount of times the student engaged in inappropriate calling out. Given such an extreme variation in scores, the teacher would probably decide to continue gathering data until a more stable trend or pattern in the behavior of concern emerges.

A second measure of central tendency is the **median**. The median marks a point in an array of data at which 50% of all the scores fall above, and 50% are below. The median is simply a measure of position. It does not tell us how large or small the data above or below are, just that 50% lies above and below. For example, Table 4.1 presents quiz scores from two different classes. Although the median score for each class is 91, the data indicate that the class performances on the quiz are certainly different in terms of variation and magnitude.

The final measure of central tendency is the **mode.** The mode is the score that occurs most frequently in a distribution. In the data presented in Table 4.1, the mode for Group 1 is 90 (with four students having this test score), whereas Group 2's mode is 98 (with two students achieving this score).

The researcher reviewing the quiz data presented in Table 4.1 has noted that although both groups have a median score of 91, Group 1 has a mode of 90, whereas Group 2's mode is 98. The researcher may wish to calculate the mean for each group. By adding the quiz scores for each student in the group and dividing by the number of scores (i.e., 9), the researcher discovers that the mean for Group 1 is 91.11, whereas Group 2's mean is 83.55. Although measures of central tendency provide valuable information about these data, no single statistic provides a complete picture of the data. As such, it is important for the teacher as action researcher to understand how to organize quantitative data using a variety of statistics to more fully describe and interpret these data.

◆ Measures of Dispersion

Though the measures of central tendency provide us with ways of knowing how the different data points cluster, in most cases there are exceptions to this statistical representation.

Clearly, not every student in Group 1 (see Table 4.1) shared the mode score of 90! But sometimes two groups of data can appear quite similar in all aspects of their central tendency and yet on closer inspection may reveal important differences. Look at the data presented in Table 4.2.

Table 4.1   Differing Data with Similar Medians

				Median				
Group 1	90	90	90	90	91	92	92	92	93
Group 2	70	73	70	60	91	97	98	95	98

Table 4.2 Similar Measures of Central Tendency with Distinct Dispersion

	Median										
Group 1	2	2	4	4	4	5	6	6	7	7	8
Group 2	0	0	2	4	4	5	6	7	8	9	10

Though it is clear that these groups of data cluster around similar measures of central tendency for both groups—modes = 4, medians = 5, and means = 5—the groups are clearly different in the degree to which individual scores vary from these measures. To gain a better understanding of the performance of these students, we need not only a measure of central tendency but also a measure of how they vary or spread out around this measure of central tendency.

There are statistical indices that describe how data vary or disperse. The most common of these measures are the **range** and the **standard deviation**.

◆ The Range

The range indicates the distance between the highest score and the lowest. For our two groups of data presented in Table 4.3, Group 1's range is 15 (i.e., highest score is 20 and lowest score is 5), whereas Group 2's range is 3 (i.e., 8 – 5).

The range is relatively simple to compute. Though it helps us to gain a more complete picture of the various data points in our collection of

Table 4.3 Similar Data, Unique Range

	Median					
Group 1	5	6	7	8	9	20
Group 2	5	6	7	8	9	8

observations, it does have its limitations. Let's return to the data presented in Table 4.3.

In this situation, although the ranges are clearly different, 15 for Group 1 (i.e., 20 – 5), and 4 for the second group (i.e., 9 – 5), the difference is a result of Group 1 having one extreme score (i.e., 20). In fact, without that score the two groups appear very much the same. The range, as a measure of variability, is susceptible to the influences of one or more extreme scores. A second measure of dispersion, which is less susceptible to this phenomenon of extreme score, is the standard deviation.

◆ The Standard Deviation

The standard deviation is a statistical measure of the spread of scores around a mean. The standard deviation attempts to remedy the influence of one extreme score by finding the average dispersion of scores as a reflection of each individual score in the array of data. With this measure in hand we now can understand where the scores typically cluster and how they typically vary about that clustering. If we describe two sets of data with the mean and standard deviation, we can begin to see how they differ from one another.

GATHERING UNDERSTANDING THROUGH QUALITATIVE DATA ANALYSIS

Qualitative researchers note that while the collection of observations, artifacts, and documents serve as valuable sources of information, the richness of that information may be lost if it is not viewed within the context of the meanings "granted them by past, present and future human agents" (Kincheloe, 1991, p. 143). Qualitative researchers believe that the human experience cannot be completely described nor understood through the exclusive use of frequencies and the process of counting, as is the case when using quantitative methods and data.

Qualitative researchers attempt to view the experience holistically, exploring all aspects, including the unique context within which the experience has occurred. Within this framework the qualitative researcher will employ a variety of methods to gather information that reflects the meaning and patterns of relationship found within a particular context of the research. Those methods involve descriptive, non-numerical collection and examination of the information.

The types of information collected in qualitative approaches are detailed, typically rich in description, and reflect in-depth inquiry (Patton, 1990). Rather than simply counting the number of times a student exhibited a particular behavior (e.g., an aggressive outburst), the teacher using a qualitative approach would attempt to provide a detailed description of the context in which the student was performing this behavior. Further, in an attempt to understand the meaning and patterns of relationship found within the context of this research, qualitative researchers may also interview students to ascertain their feelings and thoughts about the environment and their behaviors within that setting. Thus, the information collected by the qualitative researcher may include what was observed along with statements about the relationship between the observed and the values and goals of those involved. This information may take the form of direct quotes from participants as well as "field notes" reflecting the researcher's own experience. All in all, qualitative approaches and the data collected are typically context sensitive in that they provide insight into the meaningfulness and unique nature of the conditions in which the participants were engaged.

◆ Analyzing Qualitative Data

When working with potentially voluminous amounts of data gathered in qualitative research, the action researcher may at first feel somewhat overwhelmed. This can seem to be a monumental process. As one researcher noted, "The challenge is to make sense of massive amounts of data, reduce the volume of information, identify significant patterns and construct a framework for communicating the essence of what the data reveal" (Patton, 1990, pp. 371–372). There is no one commonly agreed-upon procedure for accomplishing these tasks (Best & Kahn, 1998).

Data analysis is the process of systematically organizing and presenting the findings of the action research in ways that facilitate the understanding of these data. Data analysis involves organizing and synthesizing data, finding patterns or trends in the data, and interpreting those trends. Data analysis is a series of steps to be taken, rather than one massive process.

The steps fundamental to qualitative data analysis (organize, describe, and interpret) are described in some detail below.

Organization

The first step in analyzing qualitative data is to organize the data. When the action researcher has gathered data from interviews and field notes, organizing the data may appear overwhelming. Reducing is the first step in organizing the information. The action researcher should decide upon a categorization system that allows for the grouping of data that provide similar types of information. The specifics of that system will depend on the goal of the research, the research question being studied, the setting, and the number of individuals being studied. For example, a teacher attempting to modify the behavior of a particular student may group data in categories, such as homework, essays, teacher correction, lunchroom observations, seatwork, etc.

This is not an easy task because classification systems are not automatic nor necessarily apparent in the data collected. It is important to search the data for words or phrases that reflect events and observations, which can be used to organize data. The classroom teacher may find that the original categories are too broad and that, within each, subcategories emerge. She may decide to organize her data further around themes, such as self-disclosure, cooperation, aggression, irrelevant comments, etc. These phrases could be used like labels under which data can be clustered.

Description

Following the organization and classification of the data, the action researcher should describe the salient features or characteristics of the study. This description indicates the degree to which the specific behaviors are occurring or the degree to which the specific, desired behaviors are not occurring (baseline). In Chapter 3, a case illustration was presented that focused on a teacher's frustration with cooperative groups. Assuming that the teacher, Mr. McKee, defines his concern as "a lack of student productivity while working in cooperative groups," his next step is to select a class in which this is a particular concern and to begin gathering data indicating the degree to which the groups are currently completing group assignments at an appropriate level of proficiency. These data allow the researcher to make future decisions regarding the effectiveness of the interventions used.

It is at this stage that one of the true benefits of qualitative research begins to take shape. In the case of Mr. McKee, for example, defining the problem will include answering many questions, which may include, but are not limited to the following:

1. Are the group members spending their time off task discussing upcoming weekend activities?

2. Are group members arguing with each other about the assignment?

3. Is one member "disappearing" from the group and making no contribution?

4. Is one member attempting to dominate or coerce other group members, resulting in a lack of productivity or resentment in the group?

5. How is cooperative group membership determined?

6. How are roles within the groups (researcher, recorder, narrator, etc.) determined?

7. What time of day do the most problematic groups meet?

8. What is the assignment being worked on by the group?

9. How is the activity structured? Are groups left on their own to complete large chunks of the assignment? To what degree is the teacher monitoring daily performance?

This context-driven description provides a rich presentation of a situation that cannot be obtained by simply counting the end result. These qualitative findings have direct implications for formulating the research question and the hypothesis as well as intervention development. For example, if the response to Question 5 (How is cooperative group membership determined?) indicates that students select their own group, a research question such as the following may develop: "Would the groups function more effectively if I assigned group membership based on student personality characteristics and work habits?" This research question implies that the obvious intervention is for the teacher to assign group membership in a deliberate, planned way, giving consideration to individual characteristics so as to maximize group performance. In this way, a clear description with its foundation in operational definitions drives all phases of action research, from defining the problem to evaluating outcome. Data collected at this stage may also include interview data with the students to ascertain their feelings and thoughts about the environment and their behavior within that setting. These interview data may be obtained before the intervention, during the intervention, and postintervention. Thus, the information collected by the qualitative researcher may include a description of what was observed, along with statements about the interaction between the observed, and the values and goals of those involved.

The action researcher employing qualitative data analysis describes patterns of behavior and features of the setting and context that appear to be either regularities or disruptions in regularity. Some of the descriptive material provided by our sample teacher, Mr. McKee, may include the fact that his students exhibited fluctuating attentiveness, sporadic manifestations of aggressiveness, and inconsistent work production and may elaborate on the time, place, and context of these variations in behavior.

Interpretation

The final step for the action researcher employing qualitative data analysis is to offer an interpretation of the findings. In the interpretation stage, the action researcher looks for relationships between events or behaviors, allowing meaning to emerge from the data. The researcher looks for surprises or unexpected outcomes, or what appear to be challenges to practice, as guides to the interpretative process. Mr. McKee, our sample researcher, may conclude that cooperative group performance fluctuates with time of day or group composition. Because this interpretation is affected by the researcher's background and expertise, the description of the data should be provided along with the conclusions drawn. By providing these descriptive data along with the conclusions, other reviewers can begin to understand how the conclusions were derived.

With the interpretations in hand, action researchers now begin the highly individualized process of deciding how the data will impact their practice. Will the data be shared with the student(s)? Will the research lead to a change in the teacher's practice? Do the data stimulate additional research questions? These are questions that each individual teacher turned action researcher will need to answer while analyzing the data.

ERIKSON IN ACTION: A TARGET FOR QUANTITATIVE AND QUALITATIVE DATA ANALYSIS

Although there are many developmental theories that could have been used to illustrate the value of quantitative and qualitative approaches to teacher action research, we have chosen the theory of Erik Erikson to serve as our point of illustration. It is important for the reader to understand that the current discussion of Erikson is far from comprehensive and is offered only to illustrate the process of quantitative and qualitative data analysis. Those interested in a fuller understanding of Erikson's work are referred to the readings at the end of this chapter.

Erikson believed that personality develops through eight stages or critical periods of life (Erikson, 1950). He assumed that personality develops in accordance to one's ability to interact with the environment and to resolve the conflicts or crises experienced. Given the importance of social interaction to the resolution of these developmental crises, it would appear that the effective teacher should not only understand the demands of those developmental stages but also take steps to establish a learning environment that responds to the psychosocial needs as a way of facilitating learning. Further, having implemented those steps, action researchers will want to develop quantitative and qualitative methods to validate the effectiveness of their decisions.

Though Erickson discussed eight stages of development carrying one from birth to death, the first five of these stages appear to have special import for the classroom teacher and as such are briefly described below along with possible implications for the teacher as action researcher.

◆ Stage 1: Trust versus Mistrust

The need to develop a sense of predictability about our surroundings so that we can **trust** and not fear is, for Erikson, the essential first task for each of us to accomplish as we develop a self-identity. Being able to feel safe within our environment is essential if we are to venture out and to begin to test our abilities to experience and navigate that environment. Infants who are predictably cared for when they cry and are warmly treated by their primary caregivers will develop this sense of trust and have less fear and suspicion of others.

While the resolution of this task and the development of **basic trust** or **mistrust** will have developed prior to a child's entry into school, the effects of the resolution of this task can surely be seen in a student's response to the novel situation of a classroom. For many starting school, their fear and anxiety over what to expect can be traced to a general mistrust developed during infancy. Further, it is fair to assume that, should a sense of fear and mistrust dominate a student's experience within a classroom, the willingness of that child to risk and participate and ability to attend and learn will be greatly impaired.

As action researchers, as concerned professionals, teachers need to test the conditions within their classrooms that can facilitate the development of trust within their students. We can find some direction for our decisions in Erikson's theory.

Erikson posited that basic trust is developed with consistency of care and predictability of life experiences. Although a lifetime of mistrust is difficult to overturn, it could be assumed, and therefore tested by way of action research, that students can learn to discern that in the classroom they can *trust* that they are in a safe and caring place.

With this as a starting point, teacher-researchers may question the degree to which they use predictable, consistent routines and consequences as well as the degree to which these facilitate the development of trust within that classroom. Some of the possible questions the action researcher may want to investigate, along with samples of data that could be used to answer those questions, can be found in Table 4.4.

Table 4.4   Researching Trust in the Classroom

Researchable Question	Data
Are students who exhibit a sense of trust more relaxed during the first few days of a new school year in a new class?	Record the nature and extent of student self-disclosure in small group discussions during the initial week of class. Record a description of each child's body language when entering the room and initially taking his or her seat.
Is there any difference in terms of frequency of family change in living location, family members present in the household, loss, or separation in the way they interact in their cooperative work?	Maintain anecdotal notes describing the behavior of the children in one specific cooperative learning group. Interview each child in a particular cooperative learning group, asking them to describe the various changes they have experienced in their family composition, personal life, and living situations over the past ten years.
When working with a child who appears to exhibit anxiety and mistrust, can a teacher help this child attend to the lesson by writing a lesson outline and plan on the board prior to beginning the lesson?	Have the child keep a journal describing: 1. What was taught that day 2. What he or she liked and disliked 3. How the child felt (physically) during the class period 4. How the child felt (emotionally) during the class period.

◆ Stage 2: Autonomy versus Shame and Doubt

The second of Erikson's **psychosocial stages** involves children's desire to do things on their own or act autonomously. This need to become autonomous must be balanced by the reality of safety issues. Therefore, the development of **autonomy** is facilitated when the caregiver can help provide the opportunity for self-determination in an environment that is safe.

Providing opportunities for self-governance and autonomous decision making in an environment where the chance of failure is small or the experience of failure is tolerable appears to help a child develop a sense of autonomy. As such, parents who provide clothing that is easy to remove or attach (e.g., using Velcro or slip-ons) or who provide the child with resources they can use to manage their own needs (e.g., small potty or step stool) encourage and facilitate this development of autonomy.

What, therefore, might the implications be for the classroom teacher, regardless of the age of the student? Table 4.5 lists some of the possible questions the action researcher may want to investigate, along with samples of data that could be used to answer these questions.

Table 4.5   Researching Autonomy in the Classroom

Researchable Question	Data
Do children who have home responsibilities exhibit interest and ability in being self-governing?	Record the types of questions asked by students in a particular group, following the assignment of an individual learning project.
Does providing students with freedom to choose increase their interest in the learning activity?	Have students keep a journal in which they record (1) the major learning activity assigned that day, (2) what they liked and disliked about the activity, and (3) what they would suggest should be changed in that activity.
Is a student's attitude and expected level of achievement with a learning activity affected by the degree to which they are able to perform the task independent of teacher assistance?	Have the students write an essay describing their learning style, their interest in and liking of school, and the degree to which they think they will be successful in a particular task. Repeat this assessment across a variety of activities that also vary in the degree to which teacher support will be needed to perform the task.

◆ Stage 3: Initiative versus Guilt

As children become more trusting and autonomous they will want to explore and investigate their world by taking the **initiative** in seeking and resolving new challenges. In this period, children begin to ask many questions about their world. The ever present questions of "why" and "what" seem to engulf a child at this stage, as do the inquisitive behaviors that often accompany taking initiative. This is a period of time when a child may become somewhat of a risk taker. Perhaps during this period you or one of your siblings experimented with cutting your own hair (or another's), or tried to make your own breakfast or even travel down or across the street by yourself.

In situations in which a child is discouraged from taking the initiative, Erikson believed that children would develop a sense of **guilt** regarding their natural tendency to explore and investigate. Further, Erikson believed that such guilt and resistance to initiate could carry over into later years. Assuming this theory to be true, the teacher confronted by a student who developed this sense of guilt may find it difficult to have the child participate in class or risk answering or volunteering. Table 4.6 contains some of the possible questions the action researcher may want to investigate, along with samples of data that could be used to answer those questions.

Table 4.6   Researching Initiative in the Classroom

Researchable Question	Data
How does employing a discovery approach to learning affect initiative?	Keep an anecdotal record of the degree to which children exhibit a willingness to try an activity when presented in both a discovery mode and a teacher-directed mode.
What is the impact of encouraging student to first play with learning materials prior to teaching a lesson using those materials?	Keep a log recording student comments, frequency, types of questions asked, and levels of enthusiasm in class discussion for lessons that were introduced with a play period and others without such a play period.
Is more structure and direction a help or a hindrance in facilitating initiative?	Using both structured and unstructured assignments, record the type of comments made by students in their cooperative groups, as well as who spoke to whom.

◆ Stage 4: Industry versus Inferiority

As children continue to "investigate" and explore their world, simply trying new things and new approaches will not be sufficient. Developing a sense of competence or **industry** is the next major challenge in the development of our identities. Although "trying" was important during the initiative stage, now the focus is on "doing it correctly." Thus, the children who were simply thrilled to kick the ball or run around the bases or even put on a uniform will now begin to want to know who won and how they performed. The development of a sense of industry appears to require the experience of success, but a success that comes with effort. Tasks that are too easy appear to fall short of facilitating the development of a sense of industry. Similarly, the constant experience of failure due to tasks that are beyond one's capability may result in the development of a sense of **inferiority** rather than industry.

Given this perspective, you could hypothesize that presenting tasks that fall within a student's zone of proximal development (Vygotsky, 1993) not only stimulates learning (see Chapter 3) but also can foster the development of a sense of industry. Therefore, it would appear that an effective teacher structures academic tasks so that students can successfully perform the tasks with effort and minimal support, thus allowing them to perform autonomously, which enables students to take initiative and experience success, or industry. But this is just one of many points to be considered and tested by the teacher as action researcher. Some of the possible questions the action researcher may want to investigate, along with samples of data that could be used to answer these questions, can be found in Table 4.7.

Table 4.7   Researching Industry in the Classroom

Researchable Question	Data
What is the impact of within-class competition?	Keep anecdotal records of the number of children volunteering to participate in competitive (win–lose) learning activities, as well as those volunteering to engage in noncompetitive learning activities.
	Following an activity involving class competition (e.g., spelling bee, group math contest, etc.), record the comments made by the students during a free period.
What is the impact of providing students with immediate feedback regarding their level of success in a specific learning activity?	Ask students to maintain a log identifying (1) how well they are doing and (2) their attitude about the activity.
	Invite the students to check off the assignments they have completed on a sheet posted on the bulletin.

◆ Stage 5: Identity versus Role Confusion

For middle-school and high-school teachers, Erikson's fifth stage of psychosocial development can at times be painfully obvious. In this stage, adolescents struggle to resolve the question of "Who am I?" That is, as they move increasingly from their parents to peers as a point of reference, they need to understand how they are both alike and at the same time uniquely different from everyone else. This is a period of experimentation with identity. Students begin to try on different styles, different behaviors, different values and attitudes, all in an attempt to give form to their own unique identity.

The question is, What does this search for identity mean to the classroom teacher? How could knowledge that our students are inclined to experiment with personal identity give shape to our teaching decisions? Some of the possible questions the action researcher may want to investigate, along with samples of data that could be used to answer these questions, can be found in Table 4.8.

Table 4.8   Researching Identity in the Classroom

Researchable Question	Data
What impact, if any, would the following question have on the students after reading *The Grapes of Wrath*: "If you were raised in that environment with those events, how do you think you would be different?"	Have students keep logs or journals in which they write narratives reflecting what they learned by reading a specific book and how they would evaluate the assignment.
In political science class, what would be the impact of having each student take on a specific role and then argue his or her position from that role?	Maintain anecdotal recording of the types of arguments made, the length of discussion, and the emotional expression both verbally and nonverbally. Interview the students and record their responses to the question: "How would you evaluate this learning activity?"
What would the impact be on students if, following a review of the life of an American president, they were asked to compare and contrast that president's personal characteristics with their own?	Have students write narratives comparing personal traits or characteristics and then ask the students to evaluate the learning activity.

Action Research

Increasing Social Acceptance

As our schools' student populations increase their diversity, so does concern about social exclusion as well as the need to create a sense of belonging—a sense of community—within the classroom. At least that was the concern and the focus of the action research project described by Mara Sapon-Shevin, Anne Dobbelaere, Cathleen Corrigan, Kathleen Goodman, and Mary Mastin (1998). These authors were concerned about ways in which teachers and students can effectively respond to exclusion, teasing, and isolation within the classroom.

Reviewing the Literature

The authors noted that within the field of education many attempts to generate greater inclusion and social acceptance have been employed. The authors of the current study expressed a concern that the various interventions focused on the child, with little attention given to the general social context of

the classroom. As such, those interventions often result in a lack of reciprocity in relationships. The authors' approach was stimulated by the book *You Can't Say You Can't Play* (Paley, 1992), which was a report of a teacher who investigated what children thought about the rule "You can't say you can't play." She asked, Would it work? Is it fair? These questions served as the organizing structure for the study by Sapon-Shevin et al.

Testable Questions

The project was a collaborative effort between a university professor and four elementary-school teachers from Syracuse, New York. The questions to be answered were:

- Could the teacher alter the social patterns of students' interaction through use of a no-exclusion rule?

(continued on page 65)

(continued from page 64)

◆ How would implementation of a no-exclusion rule affect the students (in general) and, more specifically, children with disabilities within those classrooms?

◆ What do students understand and say about teachers' rules and their impact on social interactions?

◆ What is the actual impact of such a rule on student interactions?

Design

The "design" was flexible and "shift[ed] according to our perceptions and needs" (p. 43). Qualitative data were collected over the course of the first year by way of field notes of observations of student social interactions. During the first year, each teacher implemented a "You can't say you can't play" rule.

Results

Did the implementation of the rule make a difference? As one first grader noted:

> It changed things for the good because some people didn't play with other kids. Sometimes they didn't play with kids who wanted to play with them. . . . Now, the kids are finding out that they can have real fun with the other kids that they weren't playing with before" (p. 44).

The authors found that the results of the rule implementation varied not only "across classes but also across grade levels" (p. 43). The fourth graders, for example, focused on how the rule changed relationships and the social climate of the classroom. In an interview one fourth-grade boy explained:

> I have noticed that when someone asks if he can play, nobody ever says, "No, you can't play." They say, "Sure!" or "Yeah, you can play," or "It's a board game for only four people and he's the fifth person; he can maybe play next time," or something like that (p. 45).

But beyond the impact on the students, the teachers also discovered the importance of considering the developmental level of their students when teaching, even if what was to be taught was the "rule." For example, in the kindergarten class, the students needed to be taught how to ask another to join in. As such, the teacher employed modeling and role play to teach the students how to invite such inclusion. The first graders identified that the rule meant more people played together and that different types of people played together, and the way they talked to one another changed. The researchers found that the fourth graders were the most reluctant to embrace the rule wholeheartedly. For those students, the rule invited other concerns. The teacher discovered through reading students' journals and having classroom discussions that the students questioned whether it was right to "force" people to play with other people. They also questioned the degree to which it was fair for one fourth-grade class to have to implement the rule when another didn't. Clearly, issues of psychosocial development (Erikson, 1950) and moral perspectives (Kohlberg, 1963) must be considered when trying to implement classroom rules or affect the social climate of the classroom.

Conclusions

It appears that a primary value to the implementation of the rule was that it served as a powerful stimulus for discussion about inclusion. But the rule was not a cure-all. The teachers found that the rule alone did not significantly affect behavior. Rather, the teacher and students had to figure out *how* to include students, not just whether they should be or not. Using the data collected from student journals, observing role-playing and problem-solving activities, and holding class meetings, the four teachers found ways to assimilate the rule into classroom activities. Those data also demonstrated that teachers can affect the social climate of their classrooms and school and can challenge existing patterns of exclusion and isolation.

COOPERATIVE LEARNING EXERCISE

Researching the Stages of Initiative and Industry

Directions

The following exercise is intended to help you use qualitative data to more fully recognize the characteristics of Erikson's psychosocial stages of initiative and industry. The exercise will require you and a partner to observe two sets of two children engaged in a play activity and then interview the students following that activity.

Step 1   Gather material for finger painting. Use newspaper and finger paints. (Alternative: Use playdough, clay, or any other creative material.)

Step 2   Prior to observing and interviewing these children, you and your partner should create a list of five words or phrases that may reflect the experience of a child in the initiative stage of psychosocial development and five words or phrases that may reflect the experience of a child who is in the industry stage of psychosocial development. For example, in discussing an activity with a child in the initiative stage, you may find him using words and phrases that address the experience of doing the new activity rather than the results of that activity: "It was fun," "It was different," "I tried it," "It's messy," etc. By comparison, a child in the industry stage may use more product-focused words and phrases such as "We won," "Mine is pretty," "See what I did?" "I made . . . ," etc.

Step 3   Identify two children you feel are in the initiative stage of psychosocial development and two who you feel may be in the industry stage. Invite them to play with the creative materials.

Step 4   Split the children into two pairs for observation. Each "observer" should sit with one pair and interview that pair after allowing fifteen minutes of play activity.

Step 5   Data collection. Record your observations of the children at play. How did they approach the materials? Did they appear to have a plan? A goal? Or were they simply interacting with the materials? What, if anything, were they saying?

After approximately fifteen minutes, stop the children and ask them:

◆ What were they doing?

◆ How did they like the activity? What did they like best? Or didn't like?

◆ Would they like to do it again? Why?

Step 6   Data analysis. Along with your partner, develop a table collating your observations and interview data.

	Students in Initiative Stage	Students in Industry Stage
Play Behaviors		
Interview Responses		

Step 7   Conclusions and reflections. Did you find any clear distinctions in the play behaviors or the students' self-reports? Were the differences reflective of the students' predicted stage of psycho-emotional development? If not, why? What could you do to improve the validity of this study? The value and validity of the data you collected?

What would you expect to happen if you asked all four students to produce a product? Or told them to simply "experience" the material and *not* make anything? Do you think it would change their play behavior? Their attitude about the activity?

INDIVIDUAL GUIDED PRACTICE EXERCISE

Me as the Focus of a Case Study

Focus: The following exercise will help you practice gathering data from observations, artifacts, and personal reflection.

Directions

Step 1   Identify five human characteristics or values that you feel are important and feel you exhibit. For example: concern for health, charitable, kind, trustworthy, achieving, etc.

Step 2   Data gathering. Keep a journal or log book recording the activities in which you have been engaged, along with the approximate length of time you spent in each activity. Record your findings each day around the same time of day. Continue this data collection for a period of seven days.

In addition to recording descriptions of the activities in which you were engaged during the day, also record your feelings and thoughts about the day and the various experiences you had.

Imagine that you are on an archeological expedition. Look about your living space (in closets, cabinets, walls, floors, etc.). What are the things that grab your attention? Write these down!

Step 3   Data analysis. List the five characteristics or values you identified as important in Step 1. Next, review your notes listing the activities in which you have engaged, along with your feelings and thoughts about those experiences and the descriptions of the "artifacts" you found.

Group these data as evidence in support of one of the five values you identified in Step 1 using a table similar to the following.

	Example: "Caring"	Value 1	Value 2	Value 3	Value 4	Value 5
Activities	1. Volunteer as big brother					
Thoughts/feelings	1. Was very upset when I heard that my friend was fired					
Artifacts	1. Envelope for donating to children with AIDS fund					

Step 4   Conclusions. Review your data. Do they seem to support the idea that you actually live or seek those qualities or values you identified as important? If not, explain. What special insights about yourself did you gain through this process? What difficulties did you have with the data collection or the data grouping? What could be done to increase the validity of your methodology and your conclusions?

Connections

FOCUS

Considering the unique psychosocial needs of our students and finding ways to organize our classrooms and learning activities in a way that engages the student cognitively and psychosocially can be a real challenge for the classroom teacher.

DIRECTIONS

Go to the following Web site:

http://www.teachers.net

Either enter a chat room or post a request for information on the bulletin board and gather information about the following:

1. What specific strategies do the teachers use to support a child's development of trust, autonomy, initiative, industry, and ego-identity within their classrooms? What data-collection techniques do they use (e.g., observations, class discussion, student interviews, etc.) to judge the effectiveness of those strategies?

2. For those teachers who require students to journal, how do they use this information in giving shape to their teaching decisions? Could they give specific examples how a student's personal disclosure has affected the teacher's planning and decision making?

◆ Key Terms

autonomy versus shame and doubt	logical positivism	psychosocial stages
basic trust	mean	qualitative data
data	measures of central tendency	quantitative data
descriptive statistics	median	range
identity versus role confusion	mode	standard deviation
industry versus inferiority	phenomenological foundation	trust versus mistrust
initiative versus guilt	psychosocial crisis	

◆ Suggested Readings

Anderson, G. L., Herr, K., & Nihlen, A. S. (1994). *Studying your own school: An educator's guide to qualitative practitioner research*. Thousand Oaks, CA: Corwin Press.

Bogdan, R. C., & Biklen, S. K. (1998). *Qualitative research in education: An introduction to theory and methods*. Boston: Allyn & Bacon.

Hoshmand, L. T. (1994). *Orientation to inquiry in a reflective professional psychology*. Albany: State University of New York Press.

Kincheloe, J. L. (1991). *Teachers as researchers: Qualitative inquiry as a path to empowerment*. Bristol, PA: Falmer Press.

Miles, M. B., & Huberman, A. M. (1994). *Qualitative data analysis: An expanded source book* (2nd ed.). Thousand Oaks, CA: Sage.

Turiel, E. (1983). *The development of social knowledge: Morality and convention*. Cambridge, UK: Cambridge University Press.

◆ References

Best, J. W., & Kahn, J. V. (1998). *Research in education* (8th ed.). Boston: Allyn & Bacon.

Erikson, E. (1950). *Childhood and society.* New York: Norton.

Calvert, P. (1986). *Responses to guidelines for developmentally appropriate practice for young children and Montessori.* Paper presented at annual meeting of the National Association for the Education of Young Children (Washington, DC).

Kincheloe, J. L. (1991). *Teachers as researchers: Qualitative inquiry as a path to empowerment.* London: Falmer Press.

Kohlberg, L. (1963). The development of children's orientation toward moral order: Sequence in the development of human thought. *Vita Humana, 6,* 670–677.

Mason, E. J., & Bramble, W. J. (1997). *Research in education and the behavioral sciences.* Madison, WI: Brown & Benchmark.

McMillan, J. H., & Schumacher, S. (2001). *Research in education* (5th ed.). New York: Longman.

Paley, V. (1992). *You can't say you can't play.* Cambridge, MA: Harvard University Press.

Parsonson, B., & Baer, D. M. (1992). The visual analysis of data and current research into the stimuli controlling it. Pp.15–40 in T. Kratochwill & J. Leven (Eds.), *Single-case research design and analysis: New directions for psychology and education.* Hillsdale, NJ: Erlbaum.

Patton, M. Q. (1990). *Qualitative evaluation and research methods* (2nd ed.) Thousand Oaks, CA: Sage.

Phillips, D. C. (1987). *Philosophy, science and social inquiry.* New York: Pergamon Press.

Sapon-Shevin, M., Dobbelaere, A., Corrigan, C., Goodman, K., & Mastin, M. (1998). Everyone here can play. *Educational Leadership* (September), 42–45.

Vygotsky, L. (1993). *The collected works of L. S. Vygotsky.* Vol. 2 (J. Knox & C. Stevens, Trans.). New York: Plenum.

CHAPTER 5

Hypothesis Testing, Validity, and Research Design: Addressing Student Needs and Reactions

S o I have this student who simply freaks out! It is hard enough to just teach the class and try to figure out what is going on with him. Now you want me to actually plan my observations and record my findings? I'm a teacher, not an experimenter, and this classroom is anything but a sterile lab!

Though the amount of time, energy, and funds often associated with research may be beyond those of most teachers, systematically planning, observing, and recording need not require extensive assignment of resources. And contrary to the position of the teacher who introduced this chapter, each classroom is a laboratory of sort, and each teacher's decision is somewhat of an experimental process.

The question, then, is how to become both a good teacher and action researcher, collecting data that are useful and valid to teaching decisions. Some of the answers can be found in understanding and applying research design and methodology to teaching decisions.

◆ Chapter Objectives

The current chapter introduces the utility of research design as a structure for action research.

After reading this chapter, you should be able to do the following:

1 Describe what is meant by the term "research design."
2 Explain what is meant by the concepts of internal validity and external validity.
3 Describe eight threats to the internal validity of a study and three threats to the external validity of a study.
4 Discuss the process of a "case study."

HYPOTHESIS TESTING: ALL IN A DAY'S WORK?

For many teachers, the thought of developing hypotheses and testing them through the use of research and research design elicits prohibitive anxiety, conjuring images of complicated statistics, rigid procedures, and sterile interaction with students and stimulating an avoidance response in the teacher. The simple truth is that we have all functioned as researchers, experimenters, and hypothesis testers, both in our professional and private lives.

Perhaps you enjoy a good mystery or detective story. You may even have enjoyed a rousing round of the board game Clue in your younger days. As you proceeded through your mystery, you most likely began to extract certain clues from which you developed and tested your hypothesis of "who done it." Or, in the game of Clue, you probably employed a series of surgically precise and carefully delivered questions to narrow in

CONTENT MAP 5

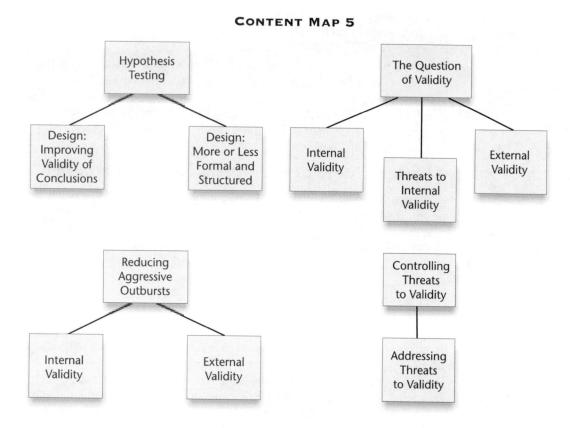

on the suspected killer, the method, and the place of the dastardly deed. In each of those experiences, you have most likely made a guess or a prediction to the answers you were seeking. Your approach to answer finding and to hypothesis testing involved a **design**, your design. If you have experienced some of the excitement of a hunt for the answer—be it in a detective story, the game of Clue, a mystery novel, or day-to-day life—the process of hypothesis testing through a research design served as a tool to assist you in finding the answers.

◆ Designs: Improving the Validity of Our Conclusions

Teachers frequently anticipate the effects of teaching decisions and strategies. Being concerned with the efficacy requires that a teacher not only anticipate the impact of decisions, but also collect data and compare the findings against those predictions. To make the connection between practice and observation, the researcher must be sure that the approach employed allows for drawing valid conclusions. It is because of this concern for validity that the action researcher must understand the nature of research design.

Heppner, Kivlighan, and Wampold (1992) describe a design as a set of procedures that reduces **error** while simultaneously helping the researcher obtain evidence about the area of interest. The error to which these authors refer would simply be any factors, other than those being investigated, which may have influenced the outcomes observed.

◆ Designs: More or Less Formal and Structured

Although it can be more or less systematic and controlled, a research design is simply the method or approach used to study areas of interest. The purpose of the design is to identify the relationship between various events occurring in the area of interest. The research design assists the researcher in connecting what has been done with the outcome observed, while at the same time ruling out as many rival explanations as possible.

Designs can range in terms of complexity, sophistication, rigidity, and control. For example, some people approach life's encounters with an air of surprise and an openness to what may come. These people employ a "design" that is flexible, more emergent, and molded by each new encounter. This is a style similar to the qualitative researcher. Even though qualitative researchers approach research with pre-planning and much forethought, they approach their research with an openness and flexibility that allows them to go where the data and the experience lead. For the qualitative researcher, it is not unusual for each incremental research decision to be shaped by the prior experience (Schumacher & McMillan, 1993). Qualitative researchers approach their research with a question in mind and the tools or strategies that will logically lead them to the answers sought. However, they do so with a flexibility that allows them to be responsive to the opportunities presented at each step along the way. It is like going on a vacation in which you know you have two weeks, will be traveling by car, have a certain amount of money to spend, and will ultimately arrive at a certain destination. But the stops in between, the routes to travel, the sites to see will be decided as you go. Although most qualitative researchers favor a flexible research design, which takes shape from the experience "as they go along" (see Janesic, 1994; Morse, 1994), some have argued for the need for qualitative researchers to employ more rigid, structured designs similar to those most often associated with quantitative methods of research (e.g., Miles & Huberman, 1994). Approaching research with more structured, fixed designs is similar to travelers, in the vacation metaphor, who know where they are heading, how long it will take, where they will stop, and what they expect to experience (as much as can be within their control) at each point of interest along the way. The design, or plan, keeps them on track, with a sense of efficiency and economy. They know what they seek, and they have designed an approach to lead them there.

The designs used must be functional and responsive to the needs and opportunities of real-world practices, while at the same time providing the structure to derive valid conclusions. Although not a slave to design, action researchers, whether employing qualitative, quantitative, or both methods, do employ designs that not only guide them through practice decisions, but also assist them in drawing valid conclusions about those decisions.

THE QUESTION OF VALIDITY

The approach, or research design, assists the researcher in applying interventions and recording outcomes and does so in ways that reduce potential error, thereby allowing the researcher to draw valid conclusions. Validity of a research design refers to two different, yet related, issues: internal and external validity.

◆ Internal Validity

Internal validity refers to the extent to which the changes in the outcome can be attributed to the introduction of the intervention or action strategy, rather than to some other factor. Internal validity refers to the degree of confidence in concluding the causal relationship among the factors researched by eliminating alternative, rival hypotheses.

Consider the situation of a teacher who believes that a student's violent classroom outbursts are the result of his frustration over his inability to perform the academic tasks presented. The teacher decides to intervene by providing the student with a peer tutor. The teacher notes a dramatic reduction in outbursts following this intervention. Although the teacher may conclude that the peer tutoring was the impetus for this change and, therefore, is an effective approach to this situation, the validity of the conclusion is only as good as the degree to which no other plausible explanation exists. Were there changes in the student's home life during this period? Did the material being taught or the manner of teaching change? Did the student's seat placement change? What effect did the attention the teacher provided to the student have on the change in behavior? Those, plus many other factors, could have accounted for the change in the student's behavior. Unless eliminated or accounted for, those rival hypotheses present error and constitute threats to the validity of the teacher's conclusions.

Threats should be anticipated and controlled for through the development and implementation of an appropriate research design prior to the implementation of the intervention. To understand the need and nature of good research designs, the action researcher needs to understand the various elements or factors that can threaten the research. Designs are developed in an attempt to reduce threats to the study's validity.

◆ Threats to Internal Validity

One model that has become a standard for conceptualizing threats to research validity was offered by Campbell and Stanley (1963), who described twelve factors that could threaten the validity of a particular research design. The action researcher who understands the nature of the threats presented below is able to develop designs that can reduce their impact and provide meaningful and valid information.

Campbell and Stanley (1963) identified eight factors that may operate within a research project and contaminate or confound the effect of the treatment. These eight threats are **history, maturation, testing, instrumentation, regression, selection, mortality,** and **selection-maturation interaction.** They reflect potential threats to the internal validity of a research study.

◆ External Validity

Studies that are internally valid demonstrate the efficacy of a particular treatment with a specific student or group of students. In addition to establishing effectiveness with a particular student or client, researchers, including action researchers, may want to demonstrate that the effectiveness of their treatment is generalizable to other students. The extent to which research findings are generalizable to a broader group marks the degree of **external validity.**

Although concern for generalization is important, it is secondary to ensuring the internal validity of the study. Internal validity is truly the sine qua non of research. Without internal validity, the research is uninterpretable (Campbell & Stanley, 1963). Certainly, generalizing information that is not valid is of little value.

For teachers concerned with the practical impact of the findings in their particular classroom, the issue of external validity typically translates into "Will these strategies work with my future students or clients?" rather than "Will this be a strategy that all teachers can use?"

The next section of this chapter addresses each of these threats along with steps a teacher as action researcher may take to reduce their potential interference.

REDUCING AGGRESSIVE OUTBURSTS: THE NEED FOR VALID INFORMATION

Mr. Walters, Bobby's fifth-grade teacher, has been frustrated and concerned about Bobby's aggressive, sometimes violent outbursts in class. Bobby has been diagnosed as having a severe attention deficit disorder, accompanied by hyperactivity. Mr. Walters has frequently sat with Bobby and explained the classroom rules about touching another student, pushing, shoving, and calling out names and threats. Bobby is very aware of what is expected, and he is also very aware of the consequences that result should these classroom rules be violated. However, his understanding of the rules and their consequences does not appear to adequately govern his behavior. Mr. Walters noted that often Bobby's behavior simply seems to come out of nowhere, unprovoked, with no apparent, identifiable cause.

After attending a workshop on aggression in the classroom, Mr. Walters began to hypothesize that Bobby's outbursts may be a reflection of his frustration over the academic work presented. To test this hypothesis Mr. Walters decided to move the children to cooperative groups in which students with a variety of academic strengths would be paired to work on the class assignments. He thought that with this peer support, the frustration Bobby was experiencing may diminish along with the violent outbursts. But what alternative explanations may be posited? What elements pose threats to the validity of Mr. Walters's conclusions?

◆ Internal Threats

History

The term *history* refers to all events that occurred in addition to the treatment between two points of measurement (i.e., one occurring before treatment, one following). In this case illustration, history may be a factor if Mr. Walters collects data about the frequency of Bobby's outbursts prior to moving toward the cooperative structure and uses those data as a way of comparing and contrasting a similar frequency following the intervention. If change is noted, it may be due to factors other than the cooperative structure intervention. Moving Bobby to a different location in the classroom, away from high student traffic (such as near the pencil sharpener) or noise irritants, may have played a significant role in reducing the outbursts. Perhaps during the time in between measurements, Bobby's parents placed him on a different medication regimen or engaged him in counseling sessions. All of these intervening factors would contribute to the history threat.

The primary way to control the threat of history is to use two groups. In this case, the events that transpire between testing affect both groups equally, with the group's "history" differing only in that one received the intervention and one did not. As will be discussed later, there are ways in which the history threat can be reduced even when working with a single case study, such as the one depicted in the illustration.

Maturation

The term *maturation* refers to the processes operating within the subject that change as a direct function of time. More immediate events, such as becoming fatigued or hungry, can reflect maturational effects, as can growth or significant changes (e.g., moving into puberty). Assume that in the previous case illustration, Mr. Walters took his initial observations early in the morning and the postinterventions later in the day. It is possible that the fatigue that comes with the passing of the day influenced the data collected in the second observation. Conversely, perhaps Bobby's difficulty with adjusting in the morning was due to his biochemical makeup or perhaps the time-released nature of his medication. Changes noted may have been due to these "maturational" factors and not necessarily the treatment. Again, the design we employ should consider this potential threat and reduce its contaminating effect on the outcome of the study.

Testing

Sometimes the very fact that someone is given a test, is observed, or simply is aware that data have been collected influences that person's behavior. *Testing* refers to changes in scores that are due to simply taking the test or having the measurement taken more than once. A student may feel more comfortable the second time around, or remember something from the previous test. In the case of Bobby, perhaps the fact that Mr. Walters began to record the frequency of Bobby's outbursts may have inspired him to be more vigilant about mediating them, thus serving as the cause for the noted reduction rather than it being a result of the new cooperative classroom structure.

Instrumentation

In designs in which more than one observation is made, changes in the method or calibration of the data-collection technique—be they from fatigue as in the case of observer data collection, or from a different form of a test—represent the instrumentation threat to validity. Perhaps the observed reduction in Bobby's outbursts following the intervention was a result of Mr. Walters's reduced vigilance and accuracy of recording rather than any real, objective change.

Regression

Statistical regression refers to the statistical phenomenon in which extreme scores (either extremely high or low scores) tend to move toward the mean upon repeated testing, so that extremely high scores on a first measure often are not as high on a second, and extremely low scores tend to move up. Therefore, changes noted between two observations may reflect the impact of regression in addition to any possible treatment effect. The implication for Mr. Walters is that the decrease noted in the frequency of Bobby's outbursts may have occurred even if no particular intervention was instituted. The decrease may reflect simple variations in Bobby's behavior or regression to the more "typical" way of reacting.

Selection

When a study employs a comparison group or individual, differences which are assumed to be the result of one group or one individual receiving a treatment may in fact be the result of the selection process that produced noncomparative groups right from the beginning of the study. For example, a social studies teacher observed that the students in a class in which she used overheads as an adjunct to her lecture scored higher on the final exam, when compared with a class in which overheads were not used. In this case, without additional information regarding the composition of those two classes, it is difficult to conclude that the higher exam scores were the result of the treatment (i.e., use of overheads) because we cannot be sure that the class selected to receive the treatment was not also the class composed of higher-achieving students. Although this is not usually a concern with a single-case design (like the case with Bobby), it would be a possibility if Mr. Walters elected to compare Bobby's aggressive outbursts with another student in that class who was not moved to a cooperative group. In this case, any differences in frequency may simply reflect the differences in the two students. Having comparable subjects or equal groups is essential to reduce this selection threat.

Mortality

Again, for those studies comparing data between comparison groups, the differential rate of attrition, or loss of subjects (mortality), can lead to different group scores. Mortality, for the case presented, would constitute a threat if Bobby stopped coming to school. If this occurred, it would be absurd to suggest that the treatment had an effect on reducing the frequency of Bobby's outbursts, even though the data collected after the introduction of the treatment revealed not one single episode of

Bobby's outbursts. Being absent from the classroom during this data collection would provide a much more viable explanation to the change in the data than assuming it was a treatment effect. Although this silly and extreme example of mortality would most likely not occur, the same dramatic effect can occur if subjects whose individual scores significantly impacted the group's score or profile "drop out" (i.e., mortality) prior to the postintervention recording. In these situations, it is impossible to determine if the change in group score is a result of the treatment or a reflection of the removal of these individuals from the group data.

Selection-Maturation Interaction

When comparison groups are used, specific groups may mature at differential rates, resulting in different levels of performance on outcome measures. If a group was investigating the effect of exercise on the onset of puberty, it would not be wise to contrast a group of fourth-grade girls who received the intervention of an exercise program to fourth-grade boys who did not. If the two groups differed at the end of a year in terms of biological evidence of reaching puberty, the researcher could not conclude with any confidence that it was the exercise and not simply the process of selecting groups along gender lines that accounted for the observed differences. Because Mr. Walters was not using a comparison group in his study of Bobby, the selection-maturation issue would not be a threat. However, because Mr. Walters did make observations over two points of time, Bobby's own individual maturation may be a threat to the internal validity of the study.

◆ External Threats

Although Mr. Walters first needs to demonstrate the effectiveness of cooperative goal structures in reducing Bobby's aggressive outbursts (internal validity), he may want to use this approach with other students. To do so requires that his "study" be controlled for possible threats to external validity. Below is a brief discussion of the possible threats to a researcher's ability to generalize findings (external validity).

Interaction of Testing and Treatment

In studies involving the use of a pretest (measurement taken prior to the introduction of the intervention), the very act of collecting those scores may affect the subject's sensitivity or responsiveness to the treatment process. Because of this, subjects not receiving the pretest may have a different response to the intervention process. For example, assume that Bobby was aware that Mr. Walters was counting the frequency of his outbursts prior to moving to the cooperative groups. This awareness may have sensitized Bobby and heightened his attention and resolve to control his behavior. This awareness and resolve could inter-act with the treatment of moving toward a cooperative structure to cre-ate the observed reduction of aggressive behavior. Without the height-ened awareness and resolve, the cooperative structure may have been less effective. Under those conditions, the ability to generalize the pro-posed treatment effect of the cooperative group experience would be limited to those who encountered this heightened awareness as a result of a pretest.

The Interaction of Selection and Treatment

It may be that the unique characteristics of the subjects in the study interacted with the treatment to produce the outcome observed. If so, the results can only be generalized to those having the same unique characteristics. Therefore, even if the results of Mr. Walters's action research were internally valid, the question whether the treatment would work similarly for students of other ages or grades is unanswered. Would it work as well for females? Would it work as well for non-ADHD students or for students whose outbursts are not caused from frustra-tion? Those questions and concerns reflect the selection-and-treatment interaction threat to the study's external validity.

Reactive Arrangement

As noted previously, when discussing outcome measures (see Chapter 3), the fact that students know they are being observed or are in a research project can affect responses. That outcome may occur only when those experiencing the treatment feel that they are in a "study." For example, it is one thing to demonstrate that students who have been provided a workshop in assertiveness will stand up for their personal convictions when confronted within the confines and safety of the "workshop." It is quite another to assume that these same students and others will react the same way in less protected, less contrived environments, such as the student lounge or neighborhood. Similarly, in the case illustration, although Mr. Walters may note a significant reduction in Bobby's aggressive outbursts, he may find less supportive findings when the cooperative group structure is part of the normal classroom procedures and not part of an "experiment" to change student behavior. Students under these less than "reactive" conditions may continue to respond as they had prior to the introduction of the treatment. Under these condi-tions, the effect noted in the original study would be considered par-tially due to the reactive effect of Bobby knowing he was under study.

Multiple-Treatment Interference

If the same subjects are used with multiple treatments, any one treatment effect may be difficult to ascertain because prior treatments may have a residual effect. This is particularly a problem with interventions that remain with the subject. For example, if prior to moving toward a group cooperative structure, Mr. Walters had taught Bobby a relaxation response, even if that relaxation procedure showed no immediate impact, it is possible that the interaction of that training with the group experience contributed to the observed changes in Bobby's behavior. Under these conditions, all other subjects would have to have experienced the multiple treatments in order to gain similar results.

CONTROLLING THREATS TO VALIDITY

Although many texts provide a listing and description of the multitude of designs available to researchers attempting to control **threats to validity** (e.g., Campbell and Stanley, 1963), there are no "best designs" that can be applied by all action researchers. All research designs will have strengths and weaknesses and all will be flawed in some way. The action researcher needs to blend resources with questions to be tested. Focusing on the threats to validity and methods for addressing those threats allows the action researcher to gather meaningful and valid information.

Strengthening the link between treatment and subsequent changes (versus alternative or competing explanations) is the ultimate goal of research designs. The sample design discussed below is intended to highlight the logic of design as a tool for controlling threats to validity rather than to promote a particular design or series of designs.

◆ Addressing the Threats to Validity

Traditionally, there have been two approaches for addressing threats to a study's validity. The first way to ensure that other factors were not the cause of the outcomes observed is to "simply" eliminate all other possible factors. However, even if perfectly controlled and sterile laboratory conditions (if they could be found) allowed the researcher to control all the threats to internal validity, the ability to apply those findings outside the artificial conditions of the laboratory (external validity) would be severely limited. It is impossible for the action researcher to eliminate all possible rival hypotheses while working in the real world of the classroom. Consider the difficulties experienced by Bobby's teacher in attempting to continue running the classroom while at the same time trying to control the various possible contaminants to the study's validity. However, the fact that all factors cannot be completely eliminated does not mean that researchers will never achieve internal validity.

The second way to control for the effects of extraneous variables is to allow them to occur while developing a strategy for accounting for their effect on the outcome. When researchers demonstrate that the observed outcome differs from the anticipated outcome as the result of these other factors, they can conclude that the difference is a result of the intervention. Even if the factors affected the outcome, the fact that the outcome differs from what would be anticipated as a consequence of these factors supports the notion that the intervention or the treatment has played a role.

Researchers attempting this approach to controlling the threats to validity have typically employed a comparison or control group design. A *comparison group* is a group in which all of the factors impacting and influencing it parallels that of the group under study, except for one condition or variable; that is, the treatment group is exposed to the intervention and the comparison group is not. With a comparison group, the researcher allows all the factors to operate, notes the change in the outcome measure, and contrasts this level of change to that noted for the treatment group. If the outcome observations for these two groups differ, the inference is that it is due not to the factors that both groups experienced in common, but to the treatment that only the target group experienced.

Although the logic is simple, the application of comparison group designs may be somewhat prohibitive for the teacher as action researcher. It is clear that more user-friendly designs are needed. The following designs, which are tailored for use with one or a few students, are known as *within-subject designs* and are action researcher friendly while providing a mechanism for improving the validity of observations and conclusions.

COOPERATIVE LEARNING EXERCISE

School Board Decision

Directions

Below you will find a description of an action research project. With colleagues or classmates, read the case illustration and assume that you were a member of the school board. How would you respond to the presentation? (Some questions to guide your decision making and discussion are provided at the end of the case illustration.)

Action Research

A Pretest/Post-Test Comparison Group Design

Hardy, Armstrong, Martin, and Strawn (1996) report on a study designed to compare children's play and aggressive behavior with firearms before and after an information-based intervention. The authors were interested in testing the effectiveness of educational programs focused on the dangers of playing with guns along with simply instructing children to stay away from firearms.

The researchers studied forty-eight children who were enrolled in one of two day-care centers in an urban setting. The pairs, matched on gender and age, were then divided with one child from each pair randomly assigned to either the treatment group (that is, those receiving the educational program) or a comparison group (control group).

Pretest

Using a videotaping process as well as a one-way mirror for unobtrusive (i.e., nonreactive) observations, the children were observed at free play. Special attention was given to the frequency with which the children played with toy guns and two disarmed real handguns located in the play area. This observation (pretest) was followed one week later with the introduction to the educational intervention.

Treatment

The children in the treatment group and their parents attended a thirty-minute presentation on the dangers of firearms.

Post-Test

One week following the intervention, both groups of children were again observed in free play. The researchers recorded the frequency of gun play.

Design

The authors used a pretest/post-test random assignment comparison design (see Figure 5.1).

In addition to randomly assigning the children to either a treatment or comparison group, the children were matched on age and gender to ensure that the variables would be equally represented in both groups. This design successfully controls for the threats to internal validity.

Results

The authors noted that the children receiving the educational intervention displayed less gun play after the intervention. However, through the use of a statistical procedure known as a *repeated-measures multivariate analysis of variance,* which allowed the authors to further evaluate the differences between these two groups, they determined that the differences between the two groups were no more than that which may be expected by chance alone and therefore not statistically significant.

Although the authors failed to provide statistical support for the effectiveness of their intervention, the outcome provided the impetus for follow-up interviews (qualitative data), which provided important information. The authors found that when asked why they played with guns despite being told about the dangers, the children replied either that the other child encouraged them or that they thought it would be okay because they did not get in trouble the first time. Although the follow-up interview provided information on additional influencing factors (e.g., peers), it also pointed to a possible contamination with this type of design. During the pretest, the children were allowed to play with guns, which led them to conclude that that behavior may be okay, despite receiving the educational program the following week. In this case it is possible that pretesting had a deleterious effect interacting with the treatment, potentially reducing its effectiveness.

R	O_1	X	O_2
Randomly assigned	Pretest firearm play	Education program	Post-test firearm play
R	O_3	No treatment	O_4

Figure 5.1

Summer Rec or Summer Wreck Program?

L. B. Taylor, the director of special education for a large urban school system, wanted to develop a sophisticated summer program, including offerings in the arts, athletics, and academic enrichment, for children with learning difficulties. Each time he presented his proposed summer program to the school board it was turned down because of the associated expenses it would entail and the lack of certainty about its value.

Mr. Taylor decided to "pilot test" his idea as a way of demonstrating its usefulness, thereby building a case for receiving funding. He contacted ten parents who had children of early school age (7–11 years old) with reading disabilities. He invited them to participate in a three-week program, which he designed and provided free of charge. The program included a morning academic activity involving the use of the Internet, reading skills, an early afternoon basketball program, and a late afternoon dramatics class.

The "volunteers" participated in the three-week program. At the end of the program, Mr. Taylor gathered data and found the following:

1. The ten student participants demonstrated a positive self-concept on a survey scale that Mr. Taylor developed.

2. Each participant expressed an interest in drama, stating that they would like to continue in such a program.

3. Each participant demonstrated the ability to dribble, use two-hand passing, and shoot a layup.

With these data in hand, Mr. Taylor approached the board, seeking funding for the expansion of the program to all children identified as learning disabled in his district.

For Reflection and Discussion

1. As a school board member, what concerns would you have about Mr. Taylor's pilot?

2. What specific concerns might you have regarding the data provided to support the effectiveness of his program?

3. What concerns do you have about the generalizability of his program?

4. If Mr. Taylor asked you for a recommendation to improve his "study," what would you suggest? Why?

INDIVIDUAL GUIDED PRACTICE EXERCISE

Controlling the Threats to Internal Validity

Select one of the activities listed below, and record the impact or result of your participation in that activity. After completing the activity, review the eight threats to internal validity and identify which, if any, were possible contaminants in your study. What are the possible alternative explanations to your findings?

Research Activities

1. Perform as many push-ups as you can and record the number completed. Next, drink a large glass of water and then attempt additional push-ups. It is hypothesized that the water will reduce muscle strength and result in fewer push-ups the second time.

2. The next time you are engaged in a telephone conversation with a friend, employ minimal encouragers as your friend speaks. That is, provide few utterances such as "yes," "I see," "hmmm," "uh-huh," etc., as your friend is speaking. Record the length of time the conversation lasts. Compare the length of this conversation with the next telephone conversation you have. It is hypothesized that the use of these encouragers will increase the length of time of a telephone conversation.

3. Select a mall or shopping center where you would or could naturally pass people while simply walking from store to store. For the first ten people you pass, look them in the eye, smile, and say, "Hello." Record the number of people who say "hello" back. For the next ten people you pass, look them in the eye and say hello, but without smiling. Again, record the number of "hellos" you receive. It is hypothesized that smiling will increase the number of responses you receive.

Reflections

For the exercise you choose to perform, which of the eight threats to internal validity went uncontrolled? What modification could you make in your design to better control against the influence of these threats? Redesign your study controlling for your potential threats and apply the research again with the new design. Were the results different?

A Review of Action Research

DIRECTIONS

◆ Go to the following Web site, which is a meeting place for people engaged in action research, and post an e-mail message or participate in the online discussion:

http://www.imc.org.uk/imc/meetingplace/imc-ali-discus/index.html

FOCUS

Identify a project currently under discussion and ask the participants to help you identify the potential threats to internal and external validity that exist. Ask the discussants how the current design targets and controls specific internal and external threats.

Bring your findings back to your classmates and colleagues for discussion.

REFLECTIONS

Was there an awareness of the possible threats to validity? Was there an appreciation of the value of controlling these threats? Did the design adequately address the threats? What would you do differently?

◆ Key Terms

research design	interaction of testing and	selection-maturation interaction
error	treatment	testing
external validity	internal validity	threats to validity
history	maturation	
instrumentation	mortality	
interaction of selection and	regression	
treatment	selection	

◆ Suggested Readings

Alter, C., & Evens, W. (1990). *Evaluating your practice: A guide to self-assessment.* New York: Springer.

Campbell, D. T., & Stanley, J. C. (1963). *Experimental and quasi-experimental designs for research.* Chicago: Rand McNally.

Heppner, P. P., Kivlighan, D. M., Jr., & Wampold, B. E. (1992). *Research design in counseling.* Pacific Grove, CA: Brooks/Cole.

◆ References

Campbell, D. T., & Stanley, J. C. (1963). *Experimental and quasi-experimental designs for research*. Chicago: Rand McNally.

Hardy, M. S., Armstrong, F. D., Martin, B. L., & Strawn, K. M. (1996). A firearm safety program for children: They just can't say no. *Developmental and Behavioral Pediatrics, 17*(4), 216–221.

Heppner, P. P., Kivlighan, D. M., Jr., & Wampold, B. E. (1992). *Research design in counseling*. Pacific Grove, CA: Brooks/Cole.

Janesic, V. J. (1994). The dance of qualitative research design. Pp. 209–219 in N. K. Denzin & Y. S. Lincoln (Eds.), *Handbook of qualitative research*. Thousand Oaks, CA: Sage.

Miles, M. B., & Huberman, A. M. (1994). *Qualitative data analysis: An expanded source book* (2nd ed.). Thousand Oaks, CA: Sage.

Morse, J. M. (1994). Designing funded qualitative research. Pp. 220–235 in N. K. Denzin & Y. S. Lincoln (Eds.), *Handbook of qualitative research*. Thousand Oaks, CA: Sage.

Schumacker, S., & McMillan, J. W. (1993). *Research in education: A conceptual introduction* (3rd ed.). New York: Harper Collins.

CHAPTER 6

Case Study and Within-Subject Designs for Observing and Adjusting to Individual Uniqueness

It's almost crazy. I have kids in my class who do their homework more accurately, more efficiently, and even more neatly while sitting in front of a television. I don't get it. I was always taught you need to have a well-lit, quiet space to do homework. What gives?

Though there are few truisms in life, one that appears consistent is that individual uniqueness does exist. Many of us have been taught that learning is best achieved when a person sits at a nicely organized desk that is well lit and away from noise and distraction. Yet research emerging in the area of individual learning styles (e.g., Dunn & Dunn, 1987) suggests that there are various methods, settings, and approaches to learning that reflect individual differences and individual preferences and that matching teaching to student learning styles capitalizes on the strengths a student brings to the classroom (e.g., Dunn & Dunn, 1987; Gardner, 1995).

The teacher depicted at the beginning of the chapter is not only confused but curious. Questions such as "Is learning-style preference an important variable to consider when preparing my class?" or "How can I determine a student's preferred learning style?" or even "Is it more useful to teach from my preferred style or to that of the student's?" need to be answered to develop strategies that maximize learning through effective use of a student's unique style. The use of the case-study approach or within-subject design discussed in this chapter could assist the teacher in finding answers to these questions.

◆ Chapter Objectives

This chapter presents the value of using case studies and within-subject methodology to test hypotheses regarding the impact of specific teaching decisions. Although the target chosen for discussion is student learning styles, the within-subject design has applications for many of the questions the action researcher may wish to pursue.

After reading this chapter, you should be able to do the following:

1 Describe the process of a "case study."
2 Identify the benefits attributed to the use of a single-subject design.
3 Describe the value of individual learning styles to the enrichment of a classroom.
4 Develop a testable hypothesis using the concepts of learning style.

SINGLE-CASE DESIGNS: A TOOL FOR THE TEACHER AS ACTION RESEARCHER

Although group designs are the ones most typically employed in the arena of academic research, they may not be appropriate or possible for the teacher as action researcher. Teachers may find that the use of case

CONTENT MAP 6

```
┌─────────────────────┐                      ┌─────────────────────┐
│ Single-Subject      │                      │ The Core Ingredients│
│ Designs:            │                      │ of Within-Subject   │
│ A Tool for the      │                      │ Designs             │
│ Teacher as Action   │                      │                     │
│ Researcher          │                      │                     │
└─────────────────────┘                      └─────────────────────┘
```

Single-Subject Designs: A Tool for the Teacher as Action Researcher

- Advantages of Single-Subject Designs
- From Case Study to Within-Subject Design
- Case Studies: A Descriptive Design

Teaching to Individual Strengths and Learning Styles

- Physiological Styles
- Teaching to or from Styles
- Cognitive Styles

The Core Ingredients of Within-Subject Designs

- Baseline
- Investigative Attitude
- Repeated Measurement

studies and single-case designs offers an alternative to large-scale multiple-group research paradigms. The field nature of action research and the need for the research to have practical and oftentimes immediate impact on all participants (thus limiting the use of untreated comparison groups) support the use of single-case designs.

◆ Advantages of Single-Case Designs

Although single-case designs have limitations, for the action researcher they provide a number of advantages over large-scale research designs (see Bloom & Fischer, 1982; Bloom, Fischer, & Orme, 1993). Specifically, single-case designs allow for each of the following:

1. **Collaboration of student and teacher.** Single-case designs allow for the teacher and student to work together designing the

approach to the situation, agreeing on the nature of the problem, discussing interventions, and mutually monitoring changes.

2. **Feedback and relevance to student.** During implementation of the strategy, the single-case nature of the design facilitates ease of communication between student and teacher, along with detailed, extensive qualitative data collection to monitor the effectiveness of the strategy.

3. **Practice relevance.** Rather than gathering information about "group average responses," which may or may not reflect the performance of any one member of the group, single-case designs allow the teacher to build knowledge about specific interventions and specific student behaviors. By intensively examining individual students and individual data, details about specific processes and techniques can be considered. Individual behavior is often ignored in studies in which a large number of participants are studied and data are treated using group means.

4. **Time and cost.** The "naturalness" of intervening with a single case allows teachers to incorporate single-case studies into their classroom practice, with minimal additional costs in terms of time and resource allocation.

5. **Qualitative and quantitative methods.** Whereas qualitative data are sometimes difficult and overwhelming to collect in large-scale studies, the single-case design allows for incorporation of both qualitative and quantitative methodology, affording the teacher as action researcher the richness of the data each method provides (e.g., Edgington, 1987; Polkinghorne, 1984).

◆ Case Studies: A Descriptive Design

Often the action researcher is interested in gathering data that provide a detailed description of what happened with one student or in one setting or program. Under these conditions, the teacher would most likely be using a case-study design. The **case study** has played a significant central role in education. Its flexibility and application to a wide range of settings, processes, people, and research questions make it a very useful method for action research.

The focus of a case study is to collect complete, detailed information about an encounter. What happened, who did what to whom and when, what were the changes or effects observed? A case study is heavy in qualitative data, with extensive detailing of conditions and events and reliance on anecdotal accounts of those involved.

The process of performing a case study has been depicted using the metaphor of a funnel (Bogdan & Biklen, 1998). The case study typically starts out with a wide view and spectrum of data collection. The researcher gathers as much data as possible that describe the case, while at the same time formulating questions, modifying techniques, and refining data collection. The case study moves from an open-ended, discovery-oriented stage to a deep analysis of interactions between the factors that explain the present status or that influence observed change or growth. Data are gathered using various techniques, including direct observations, questionnaires, and interviews.

The intense study of a single individual provides a rich source of developing hypotheses about the nature and genesis of various behaviors and learning outcomes. Alter and Evens (1990) provide illustrations of the value of single-case studies across diverse clients and target problems. However, despite this rich history and broad base of application, the case study has often been viewed as inadequate as a basis for drawing scientific inferences. Critics posit that case studies lack the "control" needed to discern the relationship between the various factors operating and observed.

Using a case study approach does not demand that the researcher abandon concerns for drawing valid conclusions. As one author clearly articulates, even though the case study is not experimental research, under several circumstances it can provide very meaningful and valid information (Kazdin, 1981).

Two design questions that confront the case-study researcher concern the type of data to collect and when to collect it. Is the researcher attempting to gather data that are typical of the situation? What is the time frame from which the data will be sampled? These, like all the questions posed and decisions made during the study, must reflect the overall purpose of the research as well as the unique characteristics of the situation. Using quantitative as well as qualitative data can increase the objectivity of the information gathered and the conclusions drawn. Additionally, the use of multiple assessment or data collection can help to strengthen the internal validity of a case study. Rather than simply collecting data at a single point in time, the case-study researcher should gather continuous data as a method of demonstrating stability of the observations as well as possible trends that exist prior to and following the introduction of the treatment.

◆ From Case Study to Within-Subject Design

Although an uncontrolled case study is vulnerable to numerous rival hypotheses, a case study in the form of a within-subject design provides mechanisms for controlling threats to validity and thus provides increased support for drawing valid inferences.

THE CORE INGREDIENTS OF WITHIN-SUBJECT DESIGNS

In the upcoming chapters, three specific within-subject designs (i.e., time series, reversal, and multiple baseline) are discussed. The goal of these chapters is to emphasize design elements as opposed to promoting specific designs. In this way, teachers are encouraged to integrate those elements into their practice and create their own designs. Understanding the elements and the logic involved provides the reader with the know-how to employ within-subject research design in the classroom. Three core elements or conditions found throughout within-subject designs are presented below (Hayes, 1981).

◆ Baseline

Unlike the more traditional comparison-group designs, **within-subject designs** use the individual student as the point for comparison. Data are collected describing the target behavior *prior* to the introduction of a treatment or practice intervention. These data can reflect magnitude, frequency, duration, or simply the existence of a particular condition. The **baseline** is the point of comparison for any noted changes in the targeted behavior following the introduction of the intervention and serves as the frame of reference for evaluation (Bloom & Fischer, 1982).

In the case of a student who is not completing assignments, the teacher records the amount of homework the student completes each day *before* introducing any interventions (establishing baseline data). The teacher then begins a treatment to address the student's problem and continues to record the amount of homework completed each day. When the changes in the behavior can be connected to the introduction of the intervention, causality can be inferred.

◆ Repeated Measurement

Human behaviors show day-to-day variations or normal fluctuations, and any one measure may reflect the student at a time of unusually high or low performance. Hayes (1981) contends that it is essential to take repeated measurements of the student. Repeated measurements across time will establish a pattern, or trend, which is relatively stable and can be used to compare a new pattern following treatment. It is this stable pattern that provides the baseline, which is used to compare changes in behavior following the introduction of a treatment. Repeated and frequent measurement of responses throughout the baseline and

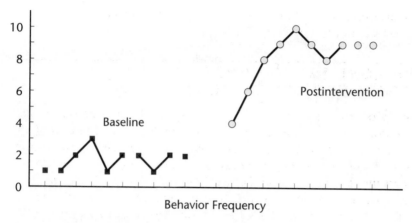

Figure 6.1 *Two-phase, or A/B design, data presentation*

intervention periods is the hallmark of single-subject and within-subject designs.

Figure 6.1 illustrates a typical graph for displaying baseline and post-intervention data. The data reflect the number of mathematics homework problems completed, out of the ten assigned each night. The multiple observations of baseline demonstrate that the behavior occurred with a frequency of approximately two times per observation period. In contrast, following the intervention, the frequency increased and stabilized at approximately nine times per observation period. The dramatic difference in patterns supports the effectiveness of the intervention.

How many measurements are needed to establish baseline? For how long should baseline data be gathered? There is no simple answer or formula for addressing those concerns. The number of observations that constitute the baseline depends on the nature of the study, the type of behavior under investigation, and the design. Barlow and Hersen (1973) suggest: "A minimum of three separate observation points, plotted on the graph, during this baseline phase are required to establish a trend in the data" (p. 320). Although this may be a guide for establishing a minimum number of observations, a more functional approach would be to collect baseline data as frequently and as long as is necessary for a stable pattern to emerge (Barlow & Hersen, 1984). Stability is assumed when the student shows a similar level of response across several observation or measurement periods. The data presented in Figure 6.2a demonstrate a student exhibiting a high degree of within-subject variability (unstable baseline). These data reflect a wide range of responses, or variability, within the individual subject across the time of observation. The variability makes the baseline data unstable and makes it difficult for the

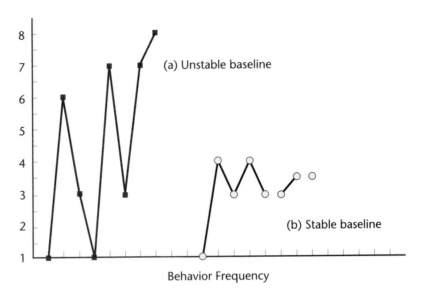

Figure 6.2 *Two samples of baseline stability*

researcher to conclude that changes in performance following the introduction of the intervention were a result of the intervention, rather than a continuation of this variability. A teacher making observations can plot the measurement points and look for flat areas in the range of observations so that connecting the plotted points provides a near horizontal line (see Figure 6.2b). The second graph of baseline data presented in Figure 6.2b demonstrates a stable baseline. In this situation a trend is clearly established, and any dramatic shift in that pattern could be assumed to have been the result of the introduction of some new factor (i.e., the intervention). Typically, it can be assumed that the more points shown within each condition (i.e., baseline and intervention), the more confidence the researcher can have in the study's conclusions (McCormick, 1994). But the primary concern remains establishing stability, rather than quantity of observation.

In addition to variability, the trend of the data must be taken into consideration when drawing conclusions. As Baer, Wolf, and Risley (1968) noted, a functional relationship can be assumed when there are systematic changes in the outcome as a result of the introduction of an intervention. However, a functional relationship cannot be shown to exist even if the subject's behaviors were changing in a direction predicted if those changes were in evidence *prior* to the introduction of the intervention. Under these conditions, it is necessary to continue collecting baseline data until a stable level is achieved.

◆ Investigative Attitude

Unlike the more rigid, controlled methods of large-scale studies, within-subject designs are intended to be dynamic and responsive to the students' needs and emerging data. The goal of these techniques is to validly assess what is happening and guide practice decisions. Hayes (1981) suggests that when unanticipated effects are recorded, the researcher must abandon the formulated design and " . . . let the client's data be the guide" (p. 197). This becomes evident when we review the use of within-subject design as applied to studying student learning styles. In order to demonstrate the application of within-subject design in service of educational research and practice, we will briefly discuss the concepts of student cognitive and learning styles and teacher response to these styles. The intent here, as with previous chapters, is to illustrate a component of educational research, rather than fully explain cognitive and learning styles. Readers interested in a more elaborate explanation of these concepts are referred to primary references listed in the reference section of this chapter.

TEACHING TO INDIVIDUAL LEARNING STYLES AND STRENGTHS

Learning styles, reflecting qualitative differences or preferences in approach to learning and performance, have been conceptualized in many different forms (Parsons, Hinson, & Brown, 2001). As you read the brief descriptions of each, ask yourself: "How would you assess your students along these dimensions?" "How would you adapt your classroom environment or your teaching strategies to engage a student's learning style?" "What impact would teaching to a student's learning style have on the student's level of achievement and attitude about herself and this class?" Those questions can be answered through the implementation of an action research design to classroom instruction.

◆ Physiological Styles

It appears that students are "wired" neurologically in ways that make information processed through some **modalities** (e.g., auditory, visual, kinesthetic, olfactory) and even under some **environmental conditions** (i.e., light, noise, temperature, etc.) easier to comprehend than if that same information was presented in a less preferred environment or through a less preferred modality (Dunn & Dunn, 1987). For example, a student who preferred to learn through hands-on experience (i.e., kinesthetic mode) in a cool, dimly lit environment may have difficulty performing in a large, bright lecture hall. Or perhaps the student who is described in the opening scene as performing more effectively in front of the television is one whose physiological preference is for environments in which there is a noisy backdrop.

◆ Cognitive Styles

Cognitive styles refers to the way a student perceives, processes, and responds to stimuli in the environment (Messick, 1994). For example, some students respond quickly in most situations, whereas others seem to take more time to reflect before responding. Consider the reactions of a student within a class when a teacher asks a question. Does the fact that some students immediately raise their hands to answer indicate they have superior knowledge, or does it reflect an **impulsive** response style? It is possible that the students who do not respond have a more **reflexive** cognitive style and are simply processing the information and making connections that require more time to respond. How would the classroom teacher know? And what are the implications for teaching? Great questions for the teacher as action researcher to pursue.

◆ Teaching to or from Style?

Because a teacher's learning style may influence his or her instructional choices, important considerations include: What happens when a teacher's learning style differs from students'? Should a teacher attempt to match instruction to students' learning styles? What may appear to be a simple yes answer is not generally agreed upon. Some believe that to do so provides a crutch to learners, enabling them to create excuses for not learning (Guild, 1994), while others say, "Yes, we should try to match styles" (Dunn & Dunn, 1987; Gardner, 1995; Shaughnessy, 1998) because by doing so, the teacher capitalizes on the diverse strengths students bring to the classroom. The question for the classroom teacher to answer is: "Is it good for *this* student, in *this* classroom?" That answer can be found when the classroom teacher becomes an action researcher and uses a within-subject design. For example, consider Case Illustration 6-1, which highlights the efforts of one teacher to increase a student's ability to complete seat work by allowing the student the freedom to move about the back of the room while he completed his work.

Not only did the teacher find a successful intervention with the student, but also she found that the collection of the data helped her to make a midprocess intervention, which helped to facilitate the final positive outcome.

COOPERATIVE LEARNING EXERCISE

Teaching Style—Student Learning Style

Directions

This task requires the use of observation and interview data. Working with a colleague, find a class in which you can observe and interview

Case Illustration 6-1
Moving to Learn

Ms. Trainer, a third-grade teacher in a suburban school system, was now into the sixth week of the new school year. She was exasperated by her inability to motivate one student, Andrew, to complete his seat work. Ms. Trainer had tried various motivational techniques, ranging from the use of incentives to the removal of recess time, all with no success.

While talking to Andrew, she realized that he did want to do the work and he was actually working on his worksheets but he always got distracted and tended to fiddle and play. So, the issue wasn't exactly motivating Andrew, but helping him to stay focused on task.

After attending a workshop on learning styles, Ms. Trainer wondered if allowing Andrew to be more mobile and to move about the room might help him focus better on completing his worksheets. She decided to test her theory using a within-subject design.

METHOD

Ms. Trainer decided to allow Andrew to complete as much of his worksheet as he was able to each day without using any artificial incentives or motivators. Each day she collected the sheets and counted the number of problems he completed. She collected *baseline* data and found that during the twenty-minute seat time, Andrew would typically complete sixty percent of the worksheets. This appeared consistent with his work, fluctuating from about fifty percent to seventy percent completion of the worksheet. Using this as a baseline, she decided to introduce the following strategy as a treatment.

TREATMENT

Ms. Trainer met with Andrew and explained that she believed that he wanted to do all his work but was having trouble staying focused for the full twenty minutes of seat work time. She said she would like to try something. She gave Andrew a clipboard to use with his worksheet and told him that when seat work time came he was to go to the desk in the back of the room. She also told Andrew that he was allowed to get out of his seat and walk back and forth across the back of the room, or simply stand up, if he wanted to. The one requirement was that while he was walking he would have to take his clipboard and try to continue working on the sheet.

DATA

Ms. Trainer continued to gather Andrew's worksheets and found the following:

Day 1 of treatment: 70% completed
Day 2 of treatment: 60% completed
Day 3 of treatment: 60% completed

MODIFICATION OF TREATMENT

Ms. Trainer noted that during the three days of "treatment," Andrew would often engage the students in the back of the class, and this talk time was interfering with his completing the worksheet. She decided to inform the class that she was trying an experiment to help Andrew finish his seat work and asked the class not to talk with Andrew during seat work time, but to keep working on their own pages. Following this class intervention, Ms. Trainer continued gathering data. Over the course of the next five days, improvement was clearly noted.

Day 4 of treatment: 80% completed
Day 5 of treatment: 100% completed
Day 6 of treatment: 100% completed
Day 7 of treatment: 100% completed
Day 8 of treatment: 100% completed

OBSERVATION

Ms. Trainer noted that not only did Andrew start to complete his work, but on the seventh and eighth day of treatment he finished his seat work in the seat and asked if he could walk only after completing the work.

both the teacher and at least five students. The task may produce more data if you can observe a class in which the teacher will be using a

Action Research

Using Learning Style and Cultural Uniqueness to Increase Interest in Technology

Maggie Steele, a classroom teacher for more than twenty-three years, taught general music in Madison, Wisconsin, elementary schools. Ms. Steele expressed frustration with her experience of having relatively few girls and minorities interacting meaningfully with computers and current technology. She describes her attempts to increase her students' level of interest and involvement in technology in an article titled "Using Music to Increase Interest in Computers for Girls and Minorities" (Steele, 1997). Not only does Ms. Steele provide an excellent example of action research as applied to issues of learning styles and cultural uniqueness, but her description of the process of formulating and implementing an action research project provides great insight into the ongoing evolving nature of a research-in-action.

Hypothesis

In reviewing her own experience with computer tutorials, Ms. Steele decided that many programs simply did not stimulate her interest or support her style of learning. She wondered if that was also the case for her students. With this question in mind, she attempted to identify features that she thought may elicit a more positive response toward computer technology from girls and minorities. Through reflection on her own experience in various classrooms and work settings, she developed a number of researchable questions:

1. Would using computers to create music increase girls' and minorities' interest in computer technology?
2. If students with a high interest in music and a low interest in computers used computers to create music, would their interest in computers increase?
3. Would integrating computer technology into a subject area (such as music) that interested many students increase their self-confidence regarding technology?

Method

As a first step to supporting her initial observations and hypothesis, Ms. Steele asked third-grade classroom teachers to identify students demonstrating high, average, or low interest in working at the computer. To cross-validate these ratings, she asked the computer expert in her school to review the third-grade population and identify those with high, average, and low interest in working at the computer. The lists were almost identical; those reported to have low interest were female and/or minority students.

Initially, Ms. Steele considered using music and nonmusic programs with the targeted individuals to see how big a factor music could be in student motivation, but time constraints didn't allow for the use of such a control technique. She employed a post-test–only, single-group approach to her investigation.

In her attempt to increase interest, Ms. Steele introduced an interactive multimedia program called "Rock, Rap 'n Roll," which provided students with the opportunity to become musical arrangers. The program was challenging for the six third-graders (two African American boys and four girls) but also rewarding. Through the use of multiple screens and mouse and keyboard interaction, students could experiment with a combination of styles, effects, instruments, and vocals to create their own musical compositions.

Results

Because Ms. Steele's goal was to tap into the musical interest of the students as a way of increasing their interest in working with computers, she gathered qualitative and quantitative data to assess the effectiveness of her instructional strategy. Ms. Steele "watched and listened to the students while they made musical choices" (p. 305) and found that the students' commitment to working on this project (because it was voluntary) was one indicator of increased interest. Further, she received reports from the classroom teachers about the excitement students expressed regarding their participation. One teacher even reported that a parent had commented about how excited her son was about this activity. A final indicator of the increased interest was that the students asked if they could spend their recess time in the "cramped, windowless closet and work at the computer" (p. 306).

At the end of the project, Ms. Steele administered a short survey to each participant asking them to evaluate their productions and their experience. As noted by the author, all of the responses were positive.

number of different teaching strategies and activities (e.g., using audio-visuals, lecturing, small group and large group discussion, hands-on learning, etc.).

Prior to Observing the Class

1. In an interview, ask the teacher to identify the learning environment and style that appears to work best for him or her. Elements could include level of noise, light, and temperature; whether the setting has to be structured and somewhat formal (desks in rows, etc.) or if it could be more informal (spread out on a bed or on the floor, etc.); and modalities (i.e., visual, auditory, kinesthetic).

2. Interview five students and identify their preferred learning environments and styles by using the same type of dimensions you used with the teacher.

Observe the Class in Action

On a sheet of paper make two columns. Label one column "Students" and the other "Teaching Activity/Environment."

Observe the five students you previously interviewed and mark your observations under the "Student" column. Look for signs of attention and active participation. For example, is the student focused on the teacher or the learning activity? Do the students appear energized, and are they participating in the learning activity (e.g., raising hands, discussing with peers, writing)?

Under the column labeled "Teaching Activity/Environment," describe what type of activity occurs during periods of high and low attention and participation.

Data Analysis

Compare your observations with those of your colleague. Did you agree on when the students were paying attention? What the high and low periods were? If not, how could your observations have been made more reliable? How would operationalizing the variables *attention, participation, high,* and *low* have helped?

Can you see any pattern between high patterns of attentiveness and student participation? Were these also reflective of the students' previously defined preferred learning styles? Did the teaching activities appear to reflect the unique demands of the material, the needs of the students, or the preferred learning style of the teacher?

Conclusions

Assume that you were the teacher of this class, now processing these data. What three modifications of your class or your teaching strategies would you begin to implement?

Also, develop a design for implementing one of the changes in teaching strategies provided for you. Use a reference point (stable baseline) to interpret the impact of your intervention.

INDIVIDUAL GUIDED PRACTICE EXERCISE

Identifying Personal Learning Styles

Focus

The following exercise is developed to help you (1) identify your own preferred learning style, (2) test the effectiveness of studying with methods reflecting that learning style, and (3) begin to identify how this may give shape to your preferred teaching activities.*

Personal Analysis of Modality Preference

Directions

Think about how each statement below applies to you. Rate the statement using: U = usually applies (3 points); S = sometimes applies (2 points); or N = never or seldom applies (1 point).

Auditory

1. While solving problems, I talk to myself or to a friend or I hum a tune.

2. During lectures in class, I can pay attention without looking at the instructor.

3. I remember material from class by repeating it orally to myself.

4. When learning something new, I like to listen to verbal explanations, records, or audiotapes.

5. I prefer to use mnemonics (or memory devices) to help me remember things from class.

*From R. D. Parsons, S. Hinson, & D. Brown (2001), Modality Preferences Inventory in *Educational psychology: A practitioner-researcher model of teaching* (Belmont, CA: Wadsworth): 185. (Used by permission.)

Visual

1. While solving problems, I take an orderly methodical approach.

2. During lectures in class, I sit near the instructor and watch intently.

3. I remember class material by picturing it in my mind.

4. When learning something new, I prefer to see it demonstrated first.

5. I find highlighting to be most helpful when I study.

6. I enjoy reading when there is a great deal of descriptive imagery.

Tactile/Haptic

1. While solving problems, I prefer to move around or pace.

2. During lectures in class, I take notes in my notebook.

3. I remember material from class that allows me hands-on experiences.

4. When learning something new, I like to try it out for myself.

5. I prefer classes with project assignments.

6. I enjoy reading stories with action scenes.

Assessment

For each category, use the number of points per response and calculate a subtotal number of points. The category of your highest subtotal is your modality of strength. It is possible to be multimodal; you may have more than one modality strength.

Developing a Within-Subject Design

Develop an action research, within-subject design that is geared to assess the effectiveness of studying in line with one's learning style preference.

Step 1. Develop an outcome measure of study effectiveness. Perhaps you could use a list of important terms from the material you will be studying and assess either the amount of study time required to understand and define those terms, or, following a given amount of study time, identify the number of words you can accurately define.

Step 2. Using a fixed amount of study time (e.g., one hour), collect the data regarding the accuracy of your term definitions for each day that you study. Record those data.

Step 3. When this baseline data appears stable, adjust your study process by incorporating techniques in line with your preferred learning style. For example, if you are an auditory learner, perhaps reading aloud or recording yourself and listening to the tape to help you study may reflect your style. Or, if you are kinesthetic, maybe copying notes or making lists would be more in line with your style preference than simply reading the material.

Step 4. Continue to assess the effectiveness of your studying using the same measure you used for your baseline. Continue collecting data for the same length of time as you did for the baseline.

Step 5. Graph your baseline and postintervention data.

Step 6. Did there appear to be a change in your data from baseline following the introduction of the intervention? If so, are there any alternative explanations other than the studying method (e.g., ease of material)? If no change was noted, give possible reasons why.

Step 7. Discuss your findings with a colleague for feedback and recommendations for design improvements.

Connections

To help you learn various ways to make your classroom and your teaching activities more culturally sensitive, go to the following multicultural education Web site:

http://www.ePALS.com

Post requests for recommendations on how teachers have modified specific course content, classroom environments, and modes of instruction to be responsive to student cultural diversity. Request information on the process and tools used to evaluate the effectiveness of these modifications. Finally, develop a design with which you could begin to implement these modifications in your classroom while at the same time gathering data that would allow you to interpret the impact of these modifications.

Reflection

How can you expand or modify these strategies so that they are effective with students whose learning style may differ from your own?

◆ Key Terms

baseline	hypothesis	modality preference
case study	impulsive	reflexive
cognitive styles	learning styles	within-subject designs
environmental conditions	modalities	

◆ Suggested Readings

Barlow, D. H. , Hayes, S. C., & Nelson, R. O. (1984). *The scientist-practitioner: Research and accountability in clinical and educational settings*. New York: Pergamon Press.

Journal of Applied Behavior Analysis. Department of Psychology, Indiana University, Bloomington, Indiana 47405. This journal provides regular illustrations of the use of within-subject designs in education and clinical practice.

Neuman, S. B., & McCormick, S. (Eds.). (1995). *Single-subject experimental research: Applications for literacy*. Newark, DE: International Reading Association.

◆ References

Alter, C., & Evens, W. (1990). *Evaluating your practice: A guide to self-assessment*. New York: Springer.

Baer, D. M., Wolf, M. M., & Risley, T. R. (1968). Some current dimensions of applied behavior analysis. *Journal of Applied Behavior Analysis, 1*(1), 91–97.

Barlow, D. H., & Hersen, M. (1973). Single case experimental design: Uses in applied clinical research. *Archives of General Psychiatry, 29*(3), 319–325.

———. (1984). *Single case experimental design: Strategies for studying behavior change* (2nd ed.). New York: Pergamon Press.

Bloom, M., & Fischer, J. (1982). *Evaluating practice: Guidelines for the accountable professional*. Englewood Cliffs, NJ: Prentice-Hall.

Bloom, M., Fischer, J., & Orme, J. (1993). *Evaluating practice: Guidelines for the accountable professional* (2nd ed.). Englewood Cliffs, NJ: Prentice-Hall.

Bogdan, R. C., & Biklen, S. K. (1998). *Qualitative research in education: An introduction to theory and methods*. Boston: Allyn & Bacon.

Dunn, K., & Dunn, R. (1987). Dispelling outmoded beliefs about student learning. *Educational Leadership, 44* (March), 55–62.

Edgington, E. S. (1987). Randomized single-subject experiments and statistical tests. *Journal of Counseling Psychology, 34*(4), 437–442.

Gardner, H. (1995). Reflection on multiple intelligences: Myths & messages. *Phi Delta Kappan, 77*, 200–210.

Guild, P. (1994). The culture/learning style connection. *Educational Leadership, 51*(8), 16–21.

Hayes, S. C. (1981). Single case experimental design and empirical clinical practice. *Journal of Counseling and Clinical Psychology, 49*(2), 193–211.

Kazdin, A. (1981). Drawing valid inferences from case studies. *Journal of Counseling and Clinical Psychology, 49*(2), 183–192.

McCormick, S. (1994). What is single-subject experimental research? In S. B. Neuman & S. McCormick (Eds.), *Single-subject experimental research: Applications for literacy*. Newark, DE: International Reading Association.

Messick, S. (1994). The matter of style: Manifestations of personality in cognition, learning and teaching. *Educational Psychologist, 29*, 121–136.

Parsons, R. D., Hinson, S., & Brown, D. (2001). *Educational psychology: A practitioner-researcher model of teaching.* Belmont, CA: Wadsworth.

Polkinghorne, D. E. (1984). Further extensions of methodological diversity for counseling psychology. *Journal of Counseling Psychology, 31*(4), 416–429.

Shaughnessy, M. E. (1998). An interview with Rita Dunn about learning styles. *Clearing House, 71*(3), 141–145.

Steele, M. (1997). Using music to increase interest in computers for girls and minorities. *Teaching and Change, 4*(4), 293–311.

THE HOW OF TEACHING: RESEARCHING LEARNING THEORY AND INSTRUCTIONAL PRACTICE

CHAPTER 7

Time Series Designs: Studying Behavior Learning Theories

You know, it is amazing. You watch the children and their behavior, their performance can be all over the place. Any one day they can be really into it, participating, right on target, and gads, other days they seem like they are in space. What makes it tough is I'm never sure if they are responding to what I'm doing or just flip-flopping on their own.

The teacher depicted in this opening vignette is clearly describing the wondrous variability of children's behavior. Though variability can certainly make life interesting for the classroom teacher, it also poses a challenge for a teacher attempting to assess the impact of a teaching strategy or teaching decision. How can a teacher be sure that the teaching strategy, or intervention, is causing the observed behavior if that behavior appears to fluctuate and change on its own?

To ensure that observed behavior is the result of a teaching decision, the action researcher must establish a stable **baseline** (a reference point) for the students' behavior before introducing a teaching intervention. After introducing the teaching strategy, the action researcher compares any observed changes against the baseline data. The current chapter presents one within-subject design that can be employed in the classroom without a large number of students as subjects or complex statistical procedures. Although these designs do require the use of systematic measurement, awareness, and specification of practice steps and consideration of design elements to guide and improve practice decisions, they can evolve into simple extensions of good rules of classroom practice.

◆ Chapter Objectives

The current chapter addresses this need and the value of establishing a comparison point, a baseline, to use as a reference. It is the first of three chapters to discuss specific within-subject designs, which provide practitioners with a quantitative, evaluative approach to assessing the impact of practice decisions. This chapter will focus on the **time series design.**

After reading this chapter, you should be able to do the following:

1   Explain what is meant by *time series design.*

2   Identify the core ingredients of a time series design as a within-subject design.

3   Explain what is meant by *baseline data* and their role in time series designs.

4   Describe how a time series design controls the threats to internal validity.

CONTENT MAP 7

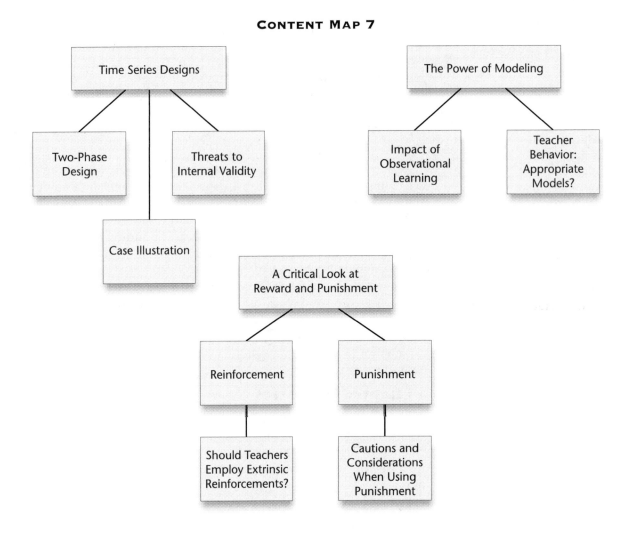

TIME SERIES DESIGNS

◆ A Valid Model for Assessing Teacher Decision Making

Although there are multiple variations on the time series design (Cook & Campbell, 1979), the most basic form is the *simple interrupted time series* (see Figure 7.1). As depicted, there are five observations ("O") both prior to and following the introduction of the treatment ("X"). Although the number of observations is equal in both pre- and post-treatment, that is not a requirement of the design.

$$O_1 \quad O_2 \quad O_3 \quad O_4 \quad O_5 \quad X \quad O_6 \quad O_7 \quad O_8 \quad O_9 \quad O_{10}$$

Figure 7.1 *Interrupted time series*

◆ Two-Phase Design

The two-phase design, often called an AB design, is the simplest form of a time series design. In phase one (A), baseline data are gathered (see observations 1–5). This baseline provides data on the targeted behavior prior to the introduction of treatment or intervention strategy. As noted above, these data become the point of comparison to demonstrate treatment effectiveness.

As with all within-subject designs, the stability of baseline data is essential. Before action researchers can conclude that a teaching strategy resulted in an observed outcome, they must be able to demonstrate not just accurate but also stable measurements of the targeted behavior during the baseline period. Certainly, a teacher who is anticipating an increase in a particular behavior may have difficulty concluding teaching effectiveness if she notices while collecting baseline data that the frequency of the behavior steadily increases. Until this increasing trend stabilizes, or flattens out, it would be hard to discern if the noted increase in behavior following the introduction of the teacher's strategy was due to that strategy, or simply a continuation of a trend started during baseline.

After obtaining baseline data, the action researcher introduces the practice steps or strategy and again collects data on the targeted behavior. These data reflect phase B (see Figure 7.1, observations 6–10). The effectiveness of the strategy is determined by a comparison of the data collected at A with that collected at B. If the stability level or trend shown in A suddenly changes when B is implemented, the inference drawn is that B (the strategy or teacher decision) was responsible for that change (see Figure 7.2).

Case Illustration 7-1 (page 112) illustrates the utility of this design for one action researcher, Ms. Linda Brennan, a third-grade teacher. As suggested by the case, the time series design requires that the action researcher take periodic measurements of the expected outcomes so that any changes that occur can be contrasted with the status before intervention. These changes can be contrasted (1) to the criterion (e.g., completing all ten problems) and (2) to the baseline level (e.g., the pattern of completing four to six problems a night). In reviewing the data, Ms. Brennan noted that Althea began to complete all ten problems (crite-

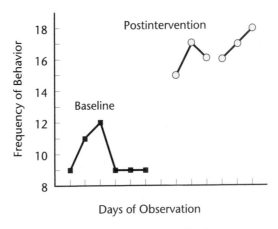

Figure 7.2 *Charting intervention effectiveness*

rion) and was more successful in homework completion than she was prior to the introduction of the intervention strategy. The apparent dramatic shift in the amount of problems completed from baseline to post-treatment provided Ms. Brennan with the evidence needed to support her conclusion that the strategy was effective.

◆ Threats to Internal Validity

As with any research design, confidence of the conclusion regarding intervention strategy causation is tempered by the degree to which the threats to internal validity were controlled. One of the factors unique to the time series design, which also increases its ability to control a variety of threats to internal validity, is the use of multiple observations

Case Illustration 7-1
Targeting Homework

Ms. Brennan, a third-grade teacher, noted that one of her students, Althea, was not completing her math problems assigned for homework. Althea always handed in something but rarely completed all ten problems that were assigned each evening. Ms. Brennan decided to see if she could improve Althea's homework production by "contracting" with her. Ms. Brennan arranged with Althea that each day she turned in all ten problems, completed and accurate, she could use the math games on the computer dur-

ing class free time, an activity Althea enjoyed. To test the effectiveness of her practice decision, Ms. Brennan checked her records on homework completion for the five-day period prior to the introduction of the contract (i.e., baseline data). She compared these data with the record of homework completion through the five days following the introduction of the computer-game contract. The data collected are represented graphically in Figure 7.3.

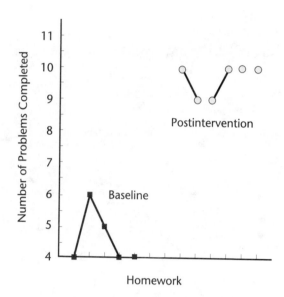

Figure 7.3 *Althea's homework production*

over time (Cook & Campbell, 1979). The use of continuous measures helps to rule out threats to internal validity, such as testing and regression, because these influences could have been noted through the multiple testing before treatment. Further, the fact that change over time can be measured (using multiple measures) implies that maturation effects can be ruled out when the post-test scores are dramatically different than any of the changes in the observations made before the intervention. One threat, which is not automatically controlled by this design, is that of history. The time period that elapsed from the pretests to the post-tests allows for the possibility that some factor or variable other than the treatment could have influenced the outcome at B. For example, what else was happening with Althea that may explain the shift in her homework behavior? Perhaps her parents started helping with the homework or maybe a brother, who was a distraction, went back to college. The less time that transpires between the pretesting and post-testing, along with efforts to maintain consistent conditions, reduces the potential effect of history on the outcome of the study.

Table 7.1 (page 114) provides a summary of the threats to internal validity that are controlled by a **repeated measures/time series design.**

Although this design certainly increases the ability to exclude alternative explanations for the occurrence of the outcomes, it is far from ideal. Some additional control against threats to validity, particularly the history threat, is desirable. The next design, the reversal or ABAB design, to be discussed in Chapter 8, addresses that concern.

Table 7.1   Internal Threats to Validity for Repeated Measures/Time Series Design

Threats to Internal Validity	Controlled by Time Series Design	Rationale
History	No	Concurrent events could occur with the treatment, which may contribute to change in data at phase B.
Maturation	Yes	Maturation does not appear to be a plausible alternative to explain a shift between O_5 and O_6 if not reflected in previous time periods under observations.
Testing	Yes	As with maturation, testing does not appear to be a plausible alternative to explain a shift between O_5 and O_6 if not reflected in previous time periods under observations.
Instrumentation	Possible, but unlikely	It would appear to be unreasonable to assume instrumentation changes occurred only at point O_6 as opposed to earlier observations.
Regression	Yes	Regression effects would be assumed to be negatively accelerated and lessening with repeated measurement. It is more likely that regression effects would be greater at the earlier observations (e.g., O_2) and thus would not be a plausible explanation for changes between O_5 and O_6.
Selection	Yes	Same person is used for comparison.
Mortality	Yes	Same person is used for comparison.
Interaction of selection and maturation, etc.	Yes	Given the control of the individual threats, interaction is unlikely. Same person is employed at baseline and post-treatment phases.

As described in Case Illustration 7-1, the use of a time series design appears effective in assessing the introduction of strategies targeted to modifying specific student behavior. For example, it appears that this design could effectively assess the impact of the selective use of rewards, punishments, and modeling on students' behavior. Each of these concepts is briefly described below. Because the focus of this chapter is on time series designs, readers interested in a more comprehensive discussion of behavioral learning theory should consult the references listed at the end of the chapter.

A CRITICAL LOOK AT REWARD AND PUNISHMENT

B. F. Skinner (1968), in his consideration of the problems of educating children, strongly encouraged teachers to make use of the principles of **operant conditioning** in their classrooms (Epstein, 1982). In fact,

Skinner suggested that teachers could be more effective if they acted as "behavioral engineers" who would observe student behavior and the **consequences** of their actions and then use these data to modify behavior. Skinner posited that the teacher as behavioral engineer could gain the type of student response desired by manipulating the consequences of a student's behavior.

◆ Reinforcement

Skinner and other operant theorists believed that the primary mechanism for changing behavior was the use of **contingency reinforcement.** Skinner contended that a behavior followed by a desired event would be strengthened or reinforced and thus increase in frequency. This strengthening would occur if the desired behavior was followed by the introduction of a pleasant, positive reinforcer. Further, the strengthening of a desired behavior would also occur if, following the occurrence of that behavior, a noxious or unpleasant stimulus was removed from the situation (i.e., negative reinforcement). Often the concepts of positive and **negative reinforcement** are mistakenly equated with reward and punishment. Both negative and **positive reinforcement** lead to increased behavior. The terms *positive* and *negative* refer to the way a stimulus works to become a reinforcer. It might be helpful to associate "positive reinforcement" with the symbol (+) as in adding, and associate "negative reinforcement" with the symbol (-) as in subtracting.

Consider the situation in which an infant cries (behavior), and in response to the cry the parent comes into the bedroom and picks up the child (a pleasant event). If the crying behavior increases in frequency, it could be assumed that it was reinforced. Further, because the consequence (i.e., being picked up) was "added" into the situation—that is, prior to crying there was no picking up, after crying picking up occurred—then this parental response acted as a positive reinforcement. Now consider what happens after the parents pick up a child (the parental behavior). If the baby stops crying (i.e., removes the crying stimulus from the situation) and if the crying was an unpleasant experience for the parent, then the removal of that crying will negatively reinforce the behavior (i.e., picking up) that resulted in the removal of this crying. In this situation, the parents have increased the baby's crying through the use of a positive reinforcement (i.e., picking up) and the baby reinforced the parents "picking up behavior" through the use of negative reinforcement (i.e., removing the crying stimulus). Did the parents know that? Did the baby? In what ways may teachers inadvertently reinforce students' behaviors that they may not want to increase? Or in what ways can they reinforce the behaviors they would like to increase? These are all questions of substance for the classroom teacher and questions that lend themselves to being investigated through action research.

◆ Should Teachers Employ Extrinsic Reinforcement?

Some argue that heavy reliance on **extrinsic rewards**—stickers, candy, movie passes, toys, etc.—results in a reduction of **intrinsic motivation** in students (Kohn, 1994). Some research (e.g., Calder & Staw, 1975; Kohn, 1993) has found that using extrinsic rewards in situations that are intrinsically interesting results in decreased motivation and interest. It is suggested (e.g., Cohen, 1985) that extrinsic rewards actually detract from learning for learning's sake. Not all agree! What do you think? How could a teacher research the effects of reinforcement on student motivation and intrinsic interest?

◆ Punishment

The use of **punishment** as a means of changing an individual's behavior or eliminating an undesirable behavior is somewhat complicated and, in most cases, ineffective unless it is used in combination with the reinforcement of an appropriate, incompatible behavior. Like reinforcement, there are two kinds of punishments: presentation and removal.

Most images of punishment evoke a situation in which a behavior results in the reception of some type of aversive stimulus (e.g., spanking, a fine, etc.). This form of punishment is called **presentation punishment.** Thus a teacher who screams at a child who is playing and not attending is attempting to employ presentation punishment (the harsh, embarrassing yell) to stop the undesirable behavior (inattentiveness). The teacher may respond to the same inattentive behavior by telling the child that he will not be allowed to go out to recess. Removing a positive event in order to reduce an undesirable behavior is called **removal punishment.**

◆ Cautions and Considerations When Using Punishment

It is important to remember that punishment controls behavior by following that behavior with aversive consequences. The use of punishment as a classroom management tool is stopgap at best and may ultimately be counterproductive in that it may cause a student to feel angry and resentful and to fall into a pattern of a power struggle with the teacher. Imagine yelling at a middle-school student who is combing her hair in class. The student, feeling embarrassed, may respond with a defiant look or comment. This teacher response and the counter-response by the student could escalate into a counterproductive exchange. Even if escalation does not occur, the teacher needs to question the student's readiness to learn following such an embarrassment.

Punishment does not change students' underlying desire nor provide guidance about what behavior to perform. If punishment is used to stop the misbehavior, the teacher must be alert to "catch the student being good" so that such appropriate behavior can be reinforced. Therefore, the child who has received a reprimand for calling out also needs to receive verbal praise as soon as he appropriately raises his hand, waits to be recognized, and then responds to the teacher's question. The combination of mild punishment with reinforcement for appropriate behavior is a strategy that may prove useful to a teacher's classroom management program, but it is also a strategy that needs to be evaluated by way of action research.

THE POWER OF MODELING

Albert Bandura (1977, 1986) examined how children learn through a process of observation. According to Bandura, much of what humans learn occurs through a process of observing and imitating others (i.e., **modeling**). Researchers have found that although there is evidence that violence on television may be modeled, this same process (observational learning) can also be a useful instructional strategy. Observational learning has been reported to enable learning-challenged preschoolers to learn basic first-aid lessons (Christensen et al., 1996), enhance learning about nature (Wilson, 1995), help teach children to play a musical instrument (Linklater, 1997; Lanners, 1999), and even prove useful in helping children who were fearful in a physical education swimming class (Weiss et al., 1998).

◆ Teacher Behavior: Appropriate Models?

The potential power of observational learning and the effects on children resulting from observing television, movies, and real adult models (including teachers) is something that needs to be considered, reviewed, and researched. Teachers serving as daily models for children in their classrooms should consider the behaviors they may be exhibiting and the impact these modeled behaviors may have on their students. For example, would a teacher who controls the class through threat and intimidation be encouraging students (through modeling) to employ these techniques of threat and intimidation to control their peers in the play yard? Or do the teacher's attitudes and behaviors toward a child with special needs set the stage for the other students to model? These are questions that need to be considered by each of us as we enter our classroom. The use of a time series design or similar within-subject design (see Chapters 8 and 9) can help the teacher draw valid conclusions concerning these and similar questions and teacher decisions.

Action Research

Parent Modeling and Increased Reading

James M. Wolf (1998), Executive Director of Synergistic Schools in Sugarland, Texas, describes an interesting example of both the modeling effect and the use of multiple observations and baseline data as a reference point to assess intervention effectiveness. The teachers in the school district were concerned about students' reading achievement and the degree to which the students engaged in independent, out-of-school reading activities.

In an action research project titled "Operation Just Read," the district began to collect data for the baseline study, using student-maintained reading logs. Data were recorded reflecting the number of books read during a week for a period of fourteen weeks. These logs were analyzed and the researchers discovered that first graders read on the average twenty-one books during this fourteen-week period, second graders thirty-five books, and third graders ten books. The researchers noted that a dramatic drop-off occurred with fourth graders, who reported an average of four books read over this fourteen-week period; fifth graders, who read three books; and sixth graders, who reported reading only three books (p. 62).

With these data as the reference point, and following a review of the literature, the researchers developed a program designed to increase the amount of independent reading. The program involved three components: (1) a continuation of the use of student reading logs; (2) a program (including forming book clubs, book trading fairs, etc.) to encourage parents and students to increase the amount of at-home reading; and (3) encouraging everyone to set goals and teachers to use charts and certificates to celebrate (reward) student progress.

Data were collected for another fourteen weeks and compared to the data collected during the fourteen-week baseline. These data are presented in Table 7.2.

As a result of the data collected over the course of the fourteen weeks of "Operation Just Read," the participants not only continued the program but expanded it to include all nine elementary schools in the district. After continuing the program for a second year with more gains in independent reading across grade levels, the researchers concluded that the home–school connection is essential to their success. They concluded that there were several necessary elements to a successful reading project. These included

1. making reading at home a schoolwide initiative with support of faculty and parents.
2. setting individual, classroom, and school goals.
3. developing a student–parent–school connection.
4. involving the parents in the process (parental modeling and reinforcement).
5. recording and analyzing the number of books read weekly (multiple recordings).
6. measuring progress in meeting the goal and publicly displaying the results.
7. celebrating progress and success (reinforcement).

Table 7.2 Comparison of Baseline and Treatment (Operation Just Read)

	Mean Number of Books Read per Grade Level During Baseline	Mean Number of Books Read after Fourteen Weeks of Operation Just Read
Grade 1	21	47
Grade 2	35	50
Grade 3	10	11
Grade 4	4	8
Grade 5	3	16
Grade 6	3	18

COOPERATIVE LEARNING EXERCISE

Time Series Observations

Directions

Below you will find examples of researchable questions, which may be of interest to a teacher. Select one and

1. identify the variable being tested.

2. operationalize that variable and define the method of data collection you would employ to assess the frequency of that variable.

3. identify a possible "treatment" or "teacher intervention" that would be introduced in order to increase this desired student behavior.

4. develop a time series design for studying the impact of this treatment.

5. discuss the possible "threats" to this design.

Example

Question: What teacher behavior would improve a specific student's participation in class?

Definition: Student participation will be defined by frequency of student hand raising in response to teacher questioning.

Treatment: When asking a question, the teacher will stand within two desk lengths from the student who is the focus of this study.

Design: Video recordings of the teacher's behavior and the student's responses will be used to gather data. For two days the teacher will teach the forty-minute class without special regard to location. For the next two days the teacher will make an effort to move closer to the student each time she poses a question to the class.

Data Analysis: The video will be reviewed and the frequency of student hand raising will be graphed for the two days prior to the change in teacher behavior and, similarly, following the change in teacher "questioning style."

Conclusions: Questions regarding stability of baseline, uncontrolled influences, etc., will be considered prior to drawing conclusions regarding the effectiveness of the "treatment."

Teacher Concerns/Researchable Questions (select one).

1. What can I do to increase Alicia's willingness to volunteer to come to the board?

2. What can I do to reduce Mary's calling out?

3. What can I do to reduce the amount of time it takes to get Richard to settle and get his materials out?

4. What can I do to increase the frequency with which Thomas completes his homework?

INDIVIDUAL GUIDED PRACTICE EXERCISE

Identifying Contingencies Controlling Behavior

Directions

Below is a list of behaviors in which you may engage daily. Select three of these behaviors, and each day for a period of one week (seven consecutive days) collect baseline data reflecting the frequency with which you demonstrate these behaviors, along with a description of the immediate consequences of engaging in these behaviors.

Develop a graph for each of these baselines that charts the daily frequency. Review each graph and identify which reflect stable baselines and which appear to either reflect extreme intrasubject variability or an unstable trend.

Identify the "reinforcers" that occur as a result of engaging in these behaviors. For example, brushing teeth is followed by a self-affirmation about your appearance; smoking a cigarette is followed by a sense of relaxation.

Sample behaviors:

1. Brushing your teeth

2. Smoking a cigarette

3. Drinking a cup of coffee (or hot tea)

4. Brushing or combing your hair

5. Answering the phone

6. Eating dessert following a meal

7. Washing your hands

8. (Any behavior of your choice)

Reflection: Select one of the above behaviors that you would like to increase or decrease in frequency. With a colleague, discuss how you may manipulate the identified consequences to modify these behaviors.

Connections

FOCUS

Aggression and violence in our schools has become an increasing area of concern for students, parents, and teachers. The focus of this Connections section is to gather information addressing strategies used to reduce violent behavior in our students.

DIRECTIONS

Go to the following Web site:

http://www.nctv.org

Gather information regarding the process of modeling and the impact that viewing aggressive behavior (either via television, movies, or real-life models such as parents or teachers) has on young viewers. What is being done within the schools to

a. educate parents and students about the possible modeling effect?

b. monitor "modeled behavior" as a source of increased aggression?

c. ensure that teachers model nonaggressive responses to conflict?

How is the effect of teacher modeling as a strategy to reduce student aggression evaluated?

◆ Key Terms

baseline
consequences
contingency reinforcement
extrinsic rewards
intrinsic motivation
modeling theory

negative reinforcement
observational learning
operant conditioning
positive reinforcement
presentation punishment
punishment

removal punishment
repeated measures
simple interrupted time series
threats to internal validity
time series design

◆ Suggested Readings

Cameron, J., & Pierce, W. D. (1996). Reinforcement, reward and intrinsic motivation: A meta-analysis. *Review of Educational Research, 64*(3), 363–423.

Chance, P. (1993). Sticking up for rewards. *Phi Delta Kappan, 74*(10), 787–790.

Neuman, S. B., & McCormick, S. (Eds.). (1995). *Single-subject experimental research: Applications for literacy.* Newark, DE: International Reading Association.

Pica, L., Jr., & Margolis, H. (1993). What to do when behavior modification is not working. *Preventing School Failure, 37*(3), 29–33.

Tracey, T. J. (1983). Single case research: An added tool for counselors and supervisors. *Counselor Education and Supervision, 22*(2), 185–196.

◆ References

Bandura, A. (1977). *Social learning theory*. Englewood Cliffs, NJ: Prentice-Hall.

————. (1986). *Social foundation of thought and action: A social cognitive theory*. Englewood Cliffs, NJ: Prentice-Hall.

Calder, B., & Staw, B. (1975). Self perception of intrinsic and extrinsic motivation. *Journal of Personality and Social Psychology, 31*(4), 599–605.

Christensen, A. M., et al. (1996). Teaching pairs of preschoolers with disabilities to seek adult assistance in response to simulated injuries: Acquisition and promotion of observational learning. *Education and Treatment of Children, 19*(1), 3–18.

Cohen, M. (1985). Extrinsic reinforcers and intrinsic motivation. Pp. 6–15 in M. Alderman & M. Cohen (Eds.), *Motivation theory and practice for preservice teachers*. Washington, DC: American Association of Colleges of Teacher Education.

Cook, T. D., & Campbell, D. T. (1979). *Quasi-experimentation: Design and analysis issues for field settings*. Boston: Houghton Mifflin.

Epstein, R. (Ed.). (1982). *Skinner for the classroom: Selected papers*. Champaign, IL: Research Press.

Kohn, A. (1994). Rewards versus learning: A response to Paul Chance. Pp. 133–136 in K. M. Cauley, F. Linder, & J. H. McMillan, *Educational psychology 94/95* (9th ed.). Guilford, CT: Dushkin Group.

————. (1993). *Punished by rewards: The trouble with gold stars, incentive plans, A's, praise and other bribes*. Boston: Houghton Mifflin.

————, & Kalat, J. W. (1992). Preparing for an important event: Demonstrating the modern view of classical conditioning. *Teaching of Psychology, 19*(2), 100–102.

Lanners, T. (1999). Teaching by example. *Clavier, 38*(5), 8–11.

Linklater F. (1997). Effects of audio- and videotape models on performance achievement of beginning clarinetists. *Journal of Research in Music Education, 45*(3), 402–414.

Skinner, B. F. (1968). *The technology of teaching*. New York: Appleton-Century-Crofts.

Weiss, M. R., McCullagh, P., & Smith, A. L. (1998). Observational learning and the fearful child: Influence of peer models on swimming skill performance and psychological responses. *Research Quarterly for Exercise and Sport, 69*(4), 380–394.

Wilson, R. (1995). Teacher as guide—The Rachel Carson way: Environmental education. *Early Childhood Education Journal, 23*(1), 49–51.

Wolf, J. M. (1998). Just Read. *Educational Leadership, 5*(8), 61–63.

Using a Reversal Design to Assess the Effectiveness of a Constructivist Approach to the Classroom

1 t was crazy, but nothing I was doing was getting the kids in my third period excited about the colonial American. I mean, they hardly volunteered answers or engaged in discussion. It was like pulling teeth. But then I started beginning class by telling a little story about Tom. He's a twelve-year-old child I made up who was living in the time of the Revolutionary War. I told this story about what he was doing on any one day, but I left the ending

hanging. When the students asked what happened, I just said, "Maybe we could figure it out after we go through today's lesson!" Gads! They loved it and were energized throughout the class. And when I stopped doing it, not only did they complain, but they went back to being lethargic. So as you can guess, the story of Tom is back in my planning and so is their enthusiasm.

Not only does the teacher depicted in the opening scenario provide a good illustration of David Ausubel's (1968) concept of **advance organizers**, but she is also illustrating the use of a **reversal** or **ABAB research design**.

As noted previously, the time series design does not control for the possibility that concurrent events (i.e., history) could occur with the treatment, which may have contributed to change in data at the intervention phase. In an attempt to reduce the threat of history and to increase the evidence of a causal connection between treatment and outcome, researchers often employ the ABAB or reversal design (Barlow & Hersen, 1984). The reversal design, like other within-subject designs, provides the classroom teacher with a quantitative, evaluative approach to assessing the impact of teaching decisions.

◆ Chapter Objectives

The reversal or ABAB design is the second of the within-subject designs to be discussed and, like the time series design (Chapter 7), can be employed in the classroom setting without the need for a large number of subjects or complex statistical procedures.

After reading this chapter, you should be able to do the following:

1 Explain what is meant by reversal/withdrawal designs.

CONTENT MAP 8

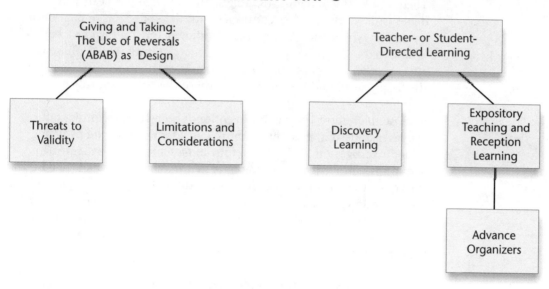

2 Describe how reversal/withdrawal designs control the threats to internal validity.

3 Identify the conditions under which reversal/withdrawal designs appear most useful and feasible.

4 Identify the key elements to discovery learning and expository teaching.

5 Describe a situation in which the impact of using an advance organizer can be studied using a reversal design.

GIVING AND TAKING: THE USE OF REVERSALS (ABAB) AS DESIGNS

As noted previously, to increase confidence in the effect of treatment, the researcher must reduce the plausibility of alternative explanations for the observed outcome, including maturation, testing, regression, and history. The reversal, or ABAB design, has been used as an extension of the time series design (Chapter 7) in order to control for the threat of history and, therefore, to increase the evidence of a causal connection between treatment and outcome (Barlow & Hersen, 1984). This design involves a modification and expansion of the basic AB design to include a replication phase, in which the researcher returns to baseline for a follow-up A phase.

The reversal design starts with a period of baseline data gathering similar to the initial phase of the AB design. After a stable baseline is achieved (A1), the intervention occurs and data are collected at B1. Then, unlike the previous AB design, once change has been successfully demonstrated, the process continues with the collection of data during a phase in which the treatment is withdrawn and a return to a baseline is observed (A2). If the treatment introduced during the B1 phase is affecting the outcomes observed, a reversal of the trend established in the B1 phase should follow the removal of the treatment (A2).

Because the removal of the intervention is an essential component of the reversal design, it is important to consider whether the behavior under investigation is likely to return to baseline levels when the intervention is removed. With treatments that may remain as residual or carryover, the return to baseline may be difficult to achieve and the interpretation of treatment effect difficult to establish. Assuming that baseline is re-established following the removal of the treatment, the final phase involves the reinstatement of intervention, with data again collected (B2).

The reversal design tests whether or not the behavior appears to be affected by the introduction and removal of the treatment. Figure 8.1 provides an illustration of the data pattern demonstrating a treatment effect.

As noted, the logic underlying this design is simple. If the changes from A1 to B1 are due to the introduction of the treatment, then removing the treatment (A2) should result in a return or near return to the previous baseline, and the re-introduction of the treatment (B2) should result in a second change in the targeted behavior. This replication process strengthens the inferred causal relationship between the observed

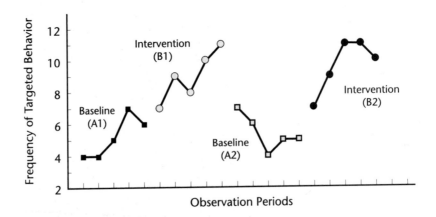

Figure 8.1 *Sample reversal: Demonstrating treatment effectiveness*

changes and the treatment process. In fact, Cook and Campbell (1979) suggested that this "design is obviously a very powerful one for inferring causal effects" (p. 222).

An illustration of a reversal design within the classroom has been presented by Roy Moxley (1998) and is summarized in Case Illustration 8-1.

Case Illustration 8-1
Treatment design

Roy Moxley (1998) presents a review of a number of research designs for use by public school teachers. The author provides a number of examples in which teachers employ treatment-only designs and student self-recordings as outcome data. In one of the studies reported, Moxley provides an illustration of one teacher's use of a reversal in testing the effect of timed writing on the number of words written by third graders.

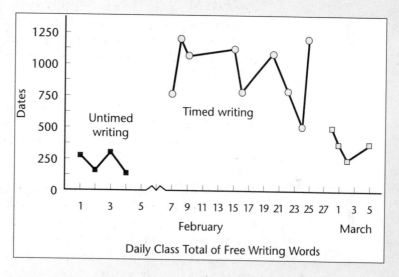

In the study, the teacher recorded the number of words written during free writing with a loose time constraint. This was followed by a period of free writing with a tight time constraint (the treatment) and then a return to the original condition of loose time constraint as base-

Figure 8.2 *Reversal design: Effect of timed writing*

line. The data presented in Figure 8.2 provide support for the effect of time constraint in increasing the number of words created during free writing.

◆ Threats to Validity

The ABAB design provides the action researcher with more controls to threats to internal validity than the simpler AB time series provides. In addition, the replication process increases the certainty that changes noted at post-treatment periods (B1, B2) are not likely to be due to the history phenomenon, because the behavior changes track the introduction and removal of the treatment across varying times.

◆ Limitations and Considerations

Although the ABAB design provides more control to threats to internal validity and increased support for inference of causality, it does have a number of problems. First, not all treatments can be withdrawn or reversed. Though the case illustration focused on a treatment that could be stopped, that is, timed or untimed writing conditions, other interventions such as providing new information or developing a student's skill cannot be removed or reversed once acquired. The teacher intending to employ a reversal design must consider the possibility of a carryover effect or a residue following the initial introduction of the teaching process or strategy. When a carryover may exist, attempts to return to baseline (A2) may not be possible, or occur only with an extended period of treatment withdrawal. Another area of concern for those using reversal designs involves the ethics of removing the intervention or treatment. If the strategy employed is apparently having a positive effect, is it ethical to withdraw the treatment at the expense of the student? The action researcher needs to consider the ethical implications of withdrawal of treatment, especially if it is possible that withdrawal can lead to harm to the student.

This was not the situation in the previous case illustration. The case illustrations in this chapter highlight the process through which the withdrawal and re-introduction of a treatment was not only possible, but provided valuable support for the teaching strategy effectiveness, without harm to the students involved. It is under these conditions (i.e., withdrawal of treatment is possible, *and* no harm will result) that withdrawal designs appear appropriate.

As with all within-subject designs, there are many variations on the fundamental design. An excellent resource for a more developed discussion of the reversal design and its variations can be found in Barlow and Hersen (1984).

TEACHER- OR STUDENT-DIRECTED LEARNING

One area in which time series designs may be of use to the action researcher is in studying the impact of specific approaches to teaching. For example, questions regarding the value or effectiveness of using teacher-directed or student-directed approaches to learning might be answered through the use of a time series design.

The following is a brief discussion of two different approaches to the learning process: **discovery learning** and **expository teaching.** The discussion is meant only as a brief introduction to these models for the purpose of illustrating the use of a time series design to test their effectiveness. Readers interested in a more detailed and comprehensive discussion of these models should consult the readings listed at the end of this chapter.

In the traditional classroom, the teacher decides which topics, concepts, and skills are to be taught and then teaches them directly and intact (Yager and Lutz, 1994). An alternative approach to learning, found in contemporary research in neuropsychology, suggests different roles for teachers and students for effective learning (Lord, 1999; Smilkstein, 1991). **Constructivism**, one of the contemporary cognitive approaches to teaching and learning, emphasizes the active role of the learner in building understanding.

The constructivist perspective emphasizes that learning occurs only when learners actively engage their cognitive structures in schema-building experiences (Yager & Lutz, 1994; Fosnot, 1996). Research suggests that three factors—**autonomy**, **interaction**, and **exploration**—are most frequently identified as characteristics of constructivist teaching and classrooms. Although constructivists support the use of these characteristics in the classroom, there is disagreement regarding the extent to which each of these factors should be emphasized. Consider the differences expressed by proponents of a discovery learning approach and those endorsing an expository teaching model.

◆ Discovery Learning

Jerome Bruner, a noted Harvard psychologist, proposed that we learn best when presented with events that stimulate insight. He believed that insightful experiences arouse interest and invoke powers of induction and translated this concept of learning through insight into a constructivist approach to teaching, identified as *discovery learning* (Bruner, 1960).

In discovery learning, teachers serve as guides. Discovery learning encourages students to make guesses based on incomplete information and stimulates them to find their own systematic means to solve problems. Bruner believed that teachers needed to nurture this intuitive thinking by encouraging students to make guesses based on incomplete evidence and then confirm or disprove the guesses systematically (Bruner, 1960). The method allows students to determine the best ways to organize new and familiar information for efficient future transfer.

However, there are questions that each teacher must answer prior to using a discovery approach to teaching. For example, in order to benefit from discovery situations, students must have basic knowledge about the problem, as well as how to apply problem-solving strategies. How can the classroom teacher know if students have these fundamentals? How does the classroom teacher work with individual differences, especially when some students have outstanding problem-solving abilities, while others may struggle? Does this method work with all levels of ability? Once these and similar issues have been addressed, the teacher can then move to the implementation of a discovery learning approach and the gathering of data, perhaps using a time series design, which then can be reviewed to determine the effectiveness of a discovery learning approach with his or her students. This is illustrated by the research presented in the action research portion of this chapter.

◆ Expository Teaching and Reception Learning

Ausubel (1968) had a different position on the process of learning. He believed that rather than acquiring knowledge through discovery, the primary mode of knowledge acquisition was through reception. He believed that if teachers do not expose students to the underlying and selective interrelationships in cognitive learning, the students may draw inappropriate conclusions. He supported an expository teaching method, requiring the teacher to provide the students with possible ways of organizing the information for more efficient encoding, storage, and retrieval. The teacher embracing an expository teaching model presents materials in a careful, organized, sequenced, and near-finished form. One of the organizing strategies offered by Ausubel was the use of **advance organizers.**

◆ Advance Organizers

Ausubel (1968) found that student learning was facilitated by providing students with deliberately prepared, slightly abstract passages in advance of the material to be learned. These advance organizers are introductory statements of a relationship or a broad concept encompassing the information to be presented. Advance organizers are presented at a slightly higher level of abstraction than students' current level of cognition (Hinson, 1988). This creates a state of cognitive disequilibrium, which, in turn, motivates the student to seek subsequent relevant information to complete the structure. This was apparent with the teacher depicted in the opening scenario. The advance organizer also serves as a **scaffold** or support for the new information about to be presented.

You may realize already that you have encountered several advance organizers in this text. The brief narrative descriptions of scenes that begin each chapter are advance organizers. You may be puzzled when you first read them, wondering what their relationship is to the subsequent content. Hopefully, the linkages become clearer as you move toward equilibrium, or understanding, of chapter content.

The general conclusions of research on advance organizers support the claim that they facilitate student learning, especially in the context of learning complex or difficult material (Corkill, 1992; Mayer 1979). There are many questions that may need to be answered before a teacher decides that advance organizers are effective for her class. Will they facilitate learning for your students? How might the subject content affect the effectiveness of advance organizers? Or, Does the age of the child limit the effectiveness or the nature of advance organizers? How about cultural variables or learning styles—how might they influence the use or the effectiveness of advance organizers? Again, these are questions that can be addressed by the action researcher. In the Cooperative Learning Section of this chapter, you will be guided in the development of an action research project using a reversal design to test the effectiveness of advance organizers.

◆ Design

The action researcher employs a time series design to assess the impact of the intervention. Given the nature of the intervention, providing the students with a new, more creative way to approach problems could not be adequately tested with a reversal design because once it was taught it could not be "untaught." However, you may want to return to this case illustration after reading the next chapter on multiple baseline designs to see if you could develop a design modification to this study, which may improve its internal validity.

COOPERATIVE LEARNING EXERCISE

Advance Organizers: Effective in Increasing Class Participation?

Purpose The following activity requires you to work with a classroom teacher to assess the effectiveness of using advance organizers to increase student participation. The exercise will require you to employ a reversal design for the action research project described on page 132.

Directions Contact a teacher who is teaching the same grade level and, or course, content that you hope to teach. With the teacher:

Step 1. Identify/define an observable behavior that could be used to assess student "in-class-participation" (e.g., asking questions, raising hand to volunteer, raising hand to respond to a question, etc.).

Action Research

Improving Mathematics Problem Solving via Discovery

K atheryn Fouche (1997) reported on an action research project conducted in eighth-grade algebra and prealgebra classes in which students were encouraged to solve non-routine mathematics problems using as many different solution strategies as possible.

Discovery Method
The research project extended over eight problem-solving sessions in which the students were given a single problem to solve individually, and then to solve in groups. The students were directed to search for as many solution methods as possible. Groups illustrated their various methods and the class discussed their experiences.

Observations
The author noted that the algebra students, who had recently learned to solve problems using simultaneous equations, tended to be fixed or stuck in applying only that procedure. The prealgebra students appeared unencumbered by such schema and employed multiple strategies including using diagrams, tables, groupings, etc.

Guided Discovery
Following these observations, the author provided guidance to the algebra students, suggesting that "they try drawing a picture" (p. 227). This scaffold appeared to open the students to the realm of vari-ous solution strategies, or as one child commented, "Oh, you didn't tell us we could do that" (p. 227). Following this intervention, the data collected revealed that the algebra students began to use a variety of problem-solving strategies.

Observations
The author observed that prealgebra students were more flexible and creative in search of problem-solving methods, a point explained by the author as a function of their not having been previously taught formal construction. It appeared that they had not developed a schema, or mental set, to approach the problem. In contrast, the algebra students tended to lock into the taught rules rather than rely on creativity and intuition. However, through guided discovery, the author was able to assist the students in progressing from a less sophisticated method to a generalization.

Conclusions
The findings of this action research project suggest that student success in algebra may be increased by having students solve problems using a variety of methods before introducing formula construction. Teaching students to develop formulas without this constructive experience may, according to this author, "leave many students with a poorly stocked problem solving 'toolbox'" (p. 229).

Step 2. Observe the students within the class for three separate days (classes). During this "baseline" period, the teacher should teach the material without the use of an advance organizer. You are to observe the students and record the frequency of in-class-participation behavior (defined in step 1) (baseline data).

Step 3. Along with the teacher, develop advance organizers to be used to introduce the material taught during the next three days (three class periods).

Step 4. Observe the students within the class for three separate days (classes). During this "treatment" period, the teacher teaches the material with the use of an advance organizer. You are to observe the students and record the frequency of in-class-participation behavior (defined in step 1) (treatment data).

Step 5. For the next three days, ask the teacher to teach the lesson without the use of an advance organizer (reversal).

Step 6. Continue to collect data as in steps 2 and 4.

Step 7. Develop a graph reflecting the data collected in steps 2, 4, and 6.

Step 8. In discussion with the classroom teacher review the graphed data.

♦ Is there an apparent change in student in-class participation associated with the presence or absence of the advance organizer?

♦ If not, does that fail to support the hypothesis that advance organizers would increase in-class participation? What else may have explained these results? For example, are observations valid? Is the baseline stable? Is there a treatment carry-over effect?

♦ If the data appear to support the hypothesized effect, what threats exist to test the validity of that conclusion (internal threats to validity)?

INDIVIDUAL GUIDED PRACTICE EXERCISE

Discovery or Expository—A Self Analysis?

Direction

Select one course in which you are currently enrolled in which the teacher uses a variety of teaching strategies (e.g., lecture, small group, cooperative group, discovery, etc.). For a period of one month, maintain a log in which you record the following data:

1. Discovery or expository? Use the following continuum to evaluate the class presentation.

    1_____10
    DISCOVERY   EXPOSITORY

2. In addition to identifying the nature of the class, record your subjective impression about your understanding of the material presented immediately following the class. Use a scale such as:

    1_____100
    CLUELESS   COMPLETE COMPREHENSION

3. After one month of collecting data, review your data. Is there a correlation between the nature of the class and your subjective feeling about your level of comprehension? What might that suggest about your preferred teaching strategies? Might the data be affected by the individual learning style of the student? The specific course content? The nature or level of complexity of the material presented? How might you design an action research project to answer these questions?

4. What might these data suggest about how you will approach your classroom instruction?

Connections

Developing Effective Expository Advance Organizers

FOCUS

This Connections is offered to assist you in developing a series of effective expository advance organizers applicable to the course or subject that you hope to teach.

DIRECTIONS

1. Go to: http://www.classroom.com

2. Click on Connected Teacher

3. Pose the following questions and requests for information:
   a. Inquire which teachers are currently teaching the grade or content level that you will someday teach.
   b. Ask those teachers if they employ expository organizers (remember: expository advance organizers provide new knowl-

edge that the student will need to understand what is about to be presented).
   c. Ask the teachers to describe those organizers.
   d. Finally, ask the teachers how they evaluate or assess the effectiveness of using those advance organizers. Do they collect data? Use action research designs?

4. How will you use this information to guide your own classroom teaching?

5. Design an action research project targeted to assess the effectiveness of advance organizers using a reversal design. Share your design with a colleague for critical review and then share your design with your online connection to see if he or she would test it out!

◆ Key Terms

ABAB research design
advance organizer
constructivist
reversal

discovery learning
expository teaching
autonomy
interaction

exploration
scaffold

◆ Suggested Readings

Dawson, V. M., & Taylor, P.C. (1998). Establishing open and critical discourses in the science classroom: Reflecting on initial difficulties. *Research in Science Education, 28*(3), 317–336.

McLean, J. E. (1995). *Improving education through action research: A guide for administrators and teachers.* Thousand Oaks, CA: Corwin Press.

Moxley, R. A. (1998). Treatment-only designs and student self-recording of strategies for public school teachers. *Education and Treatment of Children, 21*(1), 37–61.

Neuman, S. B., & McCormick, S. (Eds.). (1995). *Single-subject experimental research: Application for literacy.* Newark, DE: International Reading Association.

Zuber-Skerritt, O. (Ed.). (1996). *New directions in action research.* London: Falmer Press.

◆ References

Ausubel, D. P. (1968). *Educational psychology: A cognitive view.* New York: Holt, Rinehart & Winston.

Barlow, D. H., & Hersen, M. (1984). *Single case experimental design: Strategies for studying behavior change* (2nd ed.). Tarrytown, NY: Pergamon Press.

Bruner, J. S. (1960). *The process of education.* New York: Vintage Books.

Cook, T. D., & Campbell, D. T. (1979). *Quasi-experimentation: Design and analysis issues for field settings.* Boston: Houghton Mifflin.

Corkill, A. J. (1992). Advance organizers: Facilitators of recall. *Educational Psychology Review, 4*(1), 33–67.

Fosnot, C. T. (1996). Construction: A psychological theory of learning. In C. T. Fosnot (Ed.), *Constructivism: Theory, perspective, and practice.* New York: Teachers College Press.

Fouche, K. (1997). Algebra for everyone: Start early. *Mathematics teaching in middle schools, 2*(4), 226–230.

Hinson, S. (1988). Meaningfulness. Pp.193–210 in R. McNergney (Ed.), *Guide to classroom teaching.* Boston: Allyn & Bacon.

Lord, T. R. (1999). How to build a better mousetrap: Changing the way science is taught through constructivism. *Contemporary Education, 69*(3), 134–136.

Mayer, R. E. (1979). Can advance organizers influence meaningful learning? *Review of Educational Research, 49*(2), 371–383.

Moxley, R. A. (1998). Treatment-only designs and student self-recording of strategies for public school teachers. *Education and Treatment of Children, 21*(1), 37–61.

Smilkstein, R. (1991). A natural teaching method based on learning theory. *Gamut, 36,* 12–15.

Yager, R. E., & Lutz, M. V. (1994). Integrated science: The importance of "how" versus "what." *School Science and Mathematics, 94*(7), 338–345.

CHAPTER 9

Multiple Baseline Designs as Applied to Studying Elements of Student Motivation

1 f I heard it once, I'm sure I've heard it asked a thousand times: "Why do we have to know this?" It used to drive me crazy until I stopped and realized that it's legitimate. Why do they have to know it? You know what's amazing? Each time I would help a student see the value of what we were doing, as it applied specifically to them, they would show an enthusiasm and eagerness that made it easy to proceed.

This teacher has discovered a fundamental element of motivation. The need to see or find value in what we are doing appears fundamental to our drive and motivation to want to do it. However, valuing an activity does not appear to be sufficient for maintaining motivation. In addition to valuing an activity, it appears that we need to believe that we will be successful at the activity and that engaging in it will result in our desired outcome. Thus, the elements of "value" and "expectancy" appear pivotal to our understanding of our students' motivation to achieve at the learning tasks we provide.

As action researchers, teachers interested in identifying strategies that can be employed to maintain student motivation may find the multiple baseline design to be user-friendly and a valid approach to guiding their investigations. As such, the multiple baseline design will be the focus of this chapter.

◆ Chapter Objectives

As with the time series and reversal designs previously discussed (see Chapters 7 and 8), the multiple baseline design provides teachers with a quantitative, evaluative approach to assessing the impact of their classroom teaching decisions. The application focus for our discussion is on two elements affecting student motivation: *value* and *expectancy*.

After reading this chapter, you should be able to do the following:

1 Explain what is meant by multiple baseline designs.
2 Describe how multiple baseline designs control the threats to internal validity.
3 Design an action research project using a multiple baseline design, targeting elements of value or expectancy as a means of increasing student motivation and achievement.
4 Explain what is meant by the phrase "motivation is a function of value and expectancy."
5 Describe techniques that can increase student efficacy.

CONTENT MAP 9

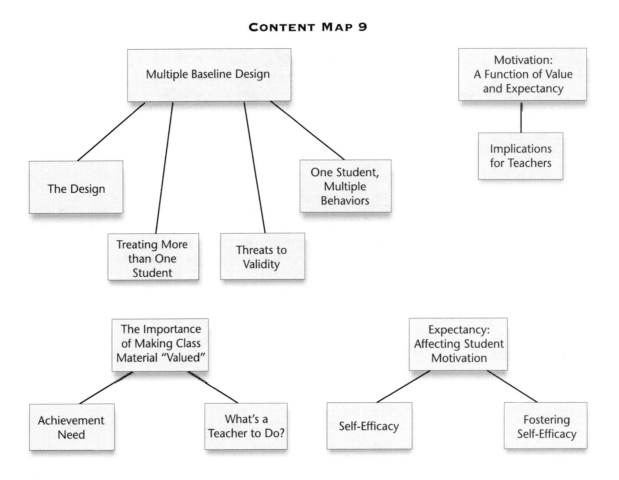

MULTIPLE BASELINE DESIGNS: ASSESSING MULTIPLE TARGETS AND INTERVENTIONS

The reversal design is certainly a useful and user-friendly design (see Chapter 8). However, as noted in Chapter 8, the utility of the reversal design may be restricted from use in some conditions. The use of sequential withdrawal of treatment, which is necessary for the reversal designs, is inappropriate when treatment variables cannot be withdrawn or reversed or the ethics of such a process may be called into question. Without this return to baseline, the effectiveness of the intervention can neither be supported nor refuted.

A related design, the multiple baseline design, extends the logic of the reversal designs just discussed. Similar to the reversal design, the multiple baseline design employs an extension of the AB design, in which baseline and subsequent treatment intervention phases are used. The multiple baseline design benefits from the same control over threats to internal validity as the AB design does. This design also controls for extraneous variables by having more than one baseline and intervention phase. However, unlike the reversal design, the multiple baseline design incorporates more than one baseline or intervention phase, without reliance on the withdrawal of the initial treatment.

◆ The Design

A multiple baseline design involves taking repeated measures of pre-intervention performance (baseline) concurrently on one variable with two or more subjects or on two or more variables within one subject. Baseline and treatment are conceptualized as separate AB designs, with the A phase (baseline) extended for each of the succeeding behaviors until the treatment condition is applied. Once stable baselines are established or the trends are predictable, the interventions are introduced, applying them to only one subject or factor at a time. As the intervention is introduced for the first target, the others remain in baseline phases. When the intervention is introduced to the second target, the third (assuming at least three students or behaviors are targeted) remains in baseline. This staggering of the treatment allows the researcher to support the prediction that the baseline data would have remained unchanged if the intervention had not been introduced. Like the logic of the reversal design, which looks for the behavior change to track the introduction of the intervention, the assumption with the multiple baseline design is that if the intervention accounts for the change in the behavior, as opposed to some extraneous factors, the behavior change will occur only at those points at which the intervention was introduced for each target. The action researcher's confidence in treatment effectiveness is increased when a change in baseline appears only after the application of the treatment, while the rate of concurrent (untreated) baselines remains relatively constant (Barlow & Hersen, 1984).

◆ Treating More than One Student

A researcher can use a multiple baseline design with two or more students who exhibit similar behaviors, or with one student who displays two or more behaviors. In this first form, in which the design is used with more than one student, logic suggests that if the behavior change occurs only at the point of the intervention for each student, then the researcher can be confident that the treatment caused the behavior change. It is assumed that the students are exposed to "identical" conditions and that it is the timing of the application of treatment that is the significant difference. The same intervention is applied to succeeding

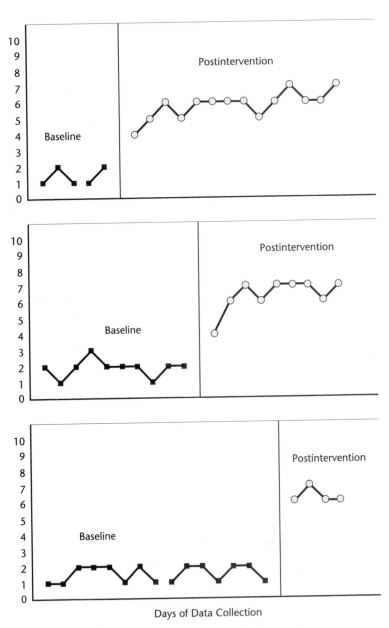

Figure 9.1 *Illustration of baseline data: Sample frequencies*

students, with the baselines of each student increasing in length, extending into the period of intervention for the other observations. Consider Figure 9.1, which offers a generic presentation of the multiple baseline design, using three separate students.

In this illustration, each student's behavior increased after the introduction of the treatment. As indicated, the researcher staggers the intervention, so the baselines for each student are different lengths. By extending the baseline for Student 2, this design controls for internal threats to validity, because the factors that could account for the change in behavior in Student 1 could reasonably be assumed to be affecting Students 2 and 3 as well, with the exception of the "treatment." The fact that the jump in behavior is evident only following the introduction of the treatment (for each student) increases the credibility of the conclusion regarding treatment effectiveness.

◆ Studying One Student but Multiple Behaviors

In addition to being used in evaluating the effectiveness of a treatment of more than one student, the multiple baseline design can be employed to study multiple behaviors of one student. In this case, data are collected on two or more student variables using the same student.

For example, a teacher may be interested in knowing the effects of using verbal praise as a way of increasing a child's participation in class by measuring the frequency with which the child asks questions and volunteers answers. Similar to the previous designs, the teacher collects baseline data and records the frequency of daily questioning and responding. After collecting the data, the teacher targets her intervention (verbal praise) to one of the specific behaviors of concern (for example, asking questions). The teacher praises the child each time the child asks a question in class and continues to collect data regarding the frequency of both forms of participation (i.e., asking and answering). The second behavior (volunteering answers) would serve as a control for the targeted behavior (asking questions). If the intervention is responsible for the noted change in the frequency of the child asking questions, then the data on volunteering answers should reveal no change during this time period. Assuming the data supported the effect of intervention on the student asking questions, the teacher could then target the verbal praise to instances when the student volunteers answers, again anticipating an increase in the frequency of responses following the introduction of the treatment.

◆ Threats to Validity

The multiple baseline design successfully controls for the internal threats to validity, as does the reversal design (Campbell & Stanley, 1963). This design, however, provides a number of benefits not previously demonstrated by the time series designs. First, when used with more than one student, the multiple baseline design allows each student the opportunity to experience the intervention. This is contrasted with the traditional comparison-group designs, which withhold treatment for the identified "control" students. A second benefit of the design is that because the treatment is introduced multiple times across time, there is an opportunity to examine both immediate effects and long-term effects of treatment. Thus, if we review the graph presented in Figure 9.1, we can see that at the time Student 3 first received treatment (i.e., short-term treatment effect), Student 1 had been receiving treatment for fourteen days (i.e., longer-term effect).

The section that follows will target elements of student motivation as they lend themselves to investigation by way of multiple baseline designs. The discussion is meant only as a brief introduction to these motivation concepts for the purpose of illustrating the use of a multiple baseline design to test the impact of its application within the classroom. Readers interested in a more detailed and comprehensive discussion of these concepts should consult the readings listed at the end of this chapter.

MOTIVATION: A FUNCTION OF VALUE AND EXPECTANCY

Feather (1982) postulated that the effort people are willing to expend on a task is a product of (a) the degree to which they value the rewards they anticipate will result from successfully completing a task and (b) the degree to which they expect to be able to perform the task successfully if they apply themselves. He suggested that motivation was the product of value multiplied by expectancy. As such, if either of these two components is missing, there will be, in effect, no motivation to engage in that particular activity.

◆ Implication for Teachers?

Using Feather's (1982) conceptualization of motivation as a reference point, the teacher confronted by an unmotivated student or class needs to question the degree to which they see and embrace the *value* of the lesson being taught. Questions such as "Why do we have to know this?" should not be dismissed. These may reflect a student's desire to value the lesson and, as a result, increase the desire (the motivation) to achieve. But as noted above, value alone is insufficient. I may value and desire to run a marathon, but know that I am in no shape to complete the race so I will be unmotivated to sign up to participate. In addition to value, people need to believe that they can perform the needed actions required to be successful. Thus, *value* without *expectancy* will result in little or no motivation to engage in the activity. Given this second element, it appears that teachers need to not only highlight the value of the learning activity, but also structure that activity in ways that make all students believe they will be successful. These elements of value and expectancy are discussed in more detail below.

◆ The Importance of Making Class Material "Valued"

One of the basic assumptions in motivation theory is that we engage in activities that appear to have value in satisfying our needs. So what need or needs may be met within the classroom, by the activities presented?

As we observe a typical class we probably could argue that students have the opportunity to meet a need for stimulation, the need to socially interact, maybe even a need to move and be physical. But how about a need to know or a desire to achieve?

◆ Achievement Need

Students who exhibit a drive to excel in learning tasks are often described as having a high achievement need (Atkinson, 1980, 1983). These are the students who persistently attempt to do well in school and succeed with high grades. These students are typically perceived as being more intrinsically motivated, ambitious, competitive, and independent in decision making than students with low needs of achievement. People with high achievement motivation generally do not require immediate gratification or rewards but can work for delayed, future rewards (Kukla, 1972). Students with a high need for achievement tend to be motivated by challenging assignments, opportunities for second attempts, and corrective feedback.

But how about students with less apparent achievement drive? It could be argued that they are being motivated by another, perhaps counter-achieving drive—that is, the need to avoid failure. These students tend to seek small, clearly defined assignments with clear, achievable payoffs.

◆ What's a Teacher to Do?

So what does the research suggest about how to motivate all students toward higher achievement?

First, it appears that students need to be assigned tasks that not only engage them at a personal level, but also are achievable (Alschuler, Tabor, & McIntyre 1971). This doesn't mean the tasks need to be easy. In fact, it appears that moderately difficult, yet doable tasks are better for stimulating achievement drive (Maehr & Sjogren, 1978).

But how about those students whose motivation to achieve is driven by the desire to avoid failure? Because research suggests that fear of failure tends to increase in strength as one's self-perception of competence declines (Eshel & Klein, 1981; Eccles, 1987), then it would follow that teachers need to provide support and praise for legitimate efforts, as well as successful outcomes, thus minimizing failure. Further, when help is needed, research has demonstrated that giving students concrete ideas about how to reach their goals increases their motivation to achieve them, whereas abstract advice (e.g., "Just keep trying") or clichéd directives ("You'll get it," "Practice makes perfect!") are not very useful (McClelland, 1985).

As with all theories, the concept of value and the role it plays in the motivation of a specific student or students needs to be assessed by each individual teacher–researcher through application of action research strategies. The use of a multiple baseline design would allow the classroom teacher to answer questions such as:

◆ "If students' physical needs are met before starting learning activities, will they value those activities more?"

◆ "Would the use of personal anecdotes or real-world examples as advance organizers increase the perceived value of the learning activity and increase student motivation?"

◆ "For students exhibiting a fear of failure, will teacher encouragement and verbal praise alone reduce their fear of failure or do these students need to experience success?"

Teachers interested in assessing the above questions could use a multiple baseline design in which one intervention is systematically introduced to a small sample of "undermotivated" students. For example, consider Case Illustration 9-1, in which a teacher uses encouragement and praise as a motivator.

EXPECTANCY: AFFECTING STUDENT MOTIVATION

Although perceiving the value of an action is a component of the motivation equation, it is only one of the components in this equation. The second ingredient essential to motivation is expectancy.

◆ Self-Efficacy

Albert Bandura (1982) suggested that an individual's beliefs (expectations) about his or her ability to reach a goal will determine how much effort is expended and how long the person will persist at goal-directed behavior. This belief about what one can and cannot do in a particular situation Bandura termed *self-efficacy*. Whether accurate or not, self-efficacy affects one's choices of activities. For example, Schunk (1990) noted, "A sense of efficacy for performing well in school may lead students to expend effort and persist at tasks, which promotes learning. As students perceive their learning progress, their initial sense of efficacy is

Case Illustration 9-1
Increasing Student Motivation

Ms. Benson, a tenth-grade language arts teacher, noted that three of her students were resistant to writing expansive, descriptive essays as part of their writing assignments. In individual conferences with these students, she found that they thought the assignments were boring, and they just wanted to get them done as fast as possible. With limited motivation, these students tended to present brief, undeveloped essays, which resulted in poor grades for the writing component of the course.

INTERVENTION

Ms. Benson decided to provide each of the three students with more individual attention, focusing on praising their efforts, pointing out well-written sections of their essays, and encouraging them (verbally) to expand on those sections.

DESIGN

Ms. Benson decided to use the word count of the essays as the data she would analyze in order to assess the effectiveness of her "motivational intervention." After a week of gathering baseline data, she began to introduce the interventions to one stu-dent at a time. For the second week, she turned her attention to Andrew, the third week to Ralph, and the fourth week of her study she focused on Mimi.

DATA

Ms. Benson noted that the students were very consistent in the length of the essays they wrote, so she felt comfortable that one week of baseline data was sufficient in getting a stable reference point. As seen in Table 9.1, all students demonstrated an increase in length of essays following the introduction of the week of individual encouragement. Further, in a follow-up interview, the students expressed more positive attitudes about the assignments and stated that they seemed less boring and more interesting to do.

CONCLUSION

Noting that the increase in word count seemed to follow the introduction of the individual encouragement, Ms. Benson began to reconfigure her classroom into small groups to facilitate her movement about the class and her ability to encourage and praise works in progress.

Table 9.1

| | Average Word Count | | | |
	WEEK 1	WEEK 2	WEEK 3	WEEK 4
Andrew	85 (baseline)	**112 (treatment)**		
Ralph	101 (baseline)	98 (baseline)	**126 (treatment)**	
Mimi	113 (baseline)	118 (baseline)	110 (baseline)	**142 (treatment)**

substantiated, which sustains motivation" (p. 33). Therefore, failure to be motivated is not always a reflection of the student's inability to see value in the activity presented. Lack of motivation can be a result of a student's strong belief that it is impossible to succeed. With this belief, the student concludes: Why try?

According to Bandura (1993), high self-efficacy is a function of a person believing (a) that he or she can successfully perform the behavior required to produce the desired outcome and (b) that the behavior will lead to the desired outcome. So, even though a student may believe that he has both the ability and the skills to study for a test, he may still lack motivation to do so if he also believes the teacher will find a way to give him an unfair test or a bad test grade.

Because feelings of efficacy motivate an individual to tackle a task, whereas feelings of inefficacy can lead to preoccupation with feelings of incompetence (Bandura, 1993; Schunk, 1990, 1995), helping students develop a sense of efficacy appears essential to effective teaching.

◆ Fostering Student Self-Efficacy

Goal setting has been identified as an important step in increasing motivation and self-efficacy in students (Locke & Latham, 1990). Goals not only give students a standard against which to measure their progress but also encourage the development of new strategies when old ones prove unsuccessful. Students who adopt learning goals, that is, goals that are focused on mastery of a task (Pintrich & Garcia, 1991), tend to persevere when encountering difficulty and focus on personal mastery rather than competition or failure avoidance (Nicholls, 1984; Stipek, 1996). However, for goals to work in this motivating manner, they need to be (1) specific, (2) close at hand, and (3) moderately difficult (Bruning, Schraw, & Ronning, 1995). Further, increased motivation appears to result more readily when the goals are developed by, and thus owned by, the student (Pintrich & Schunk, 1996; Ridley, McCombs, & Taylor, 1994). Having students set their own goals and make a commitment to try to reach those goals increases their performance (Bandura & Schunk, 1981; Tollefson et al., 1984). Questions such as the following need to be answered: "What defines appropriate learning goals for a student?" "How do students know they are making genuine progress?" "How can a teacher assess increased self-efficacy in his or her students?"

Self-efficacy theory appears to have value for the classroom teacher; however, as with all theories, the value of this one as applied to a teacher's specific classroom needs to be assessed through application of action research strategies. Ms. Benson, the teacher in Case Illustration 9-1 did exactly that, as described in Case Illustration 9-2.

Case Illustration 9-2
Increasing Homework Completion

Ms. Ginny Morton, a sixth-grade mathematics teacher, had a difficult time motivating Niki to complete homework or seat work mathematics problems. Niki rarely completed all of the problems assigned and almost never volunteered answers in class. Ms. Morton decided to use a goal-setting strategy to increase Niki's motivation to complete her assigned work, as well as to increase the frequency with which she volunteered answers.

DESIGN

Ms. Morton began her study by taking baseline data over four class periods. The consistency of Niki's performance, or lack of performance, suggested a stable baseline. During the next five days, Ms. Morton worked with Niki to set goals regarding the number of homework problems to be completed. The first goal was to complete at least 50%, then 75%, and finally 100% of the problems. At the end of each class day, Ms. Morton and Niki reviewed the number of problems and reaffirmed the next day's goal.

While these data were collected, Ms. Morton continued to observe and record the frequency with which Niki volunteered answers in class. After five days of treatment, Ms. Morton showed the data to Niki and suggested they try to set goals for responding (volunteering answers in class). Goals for volunteering were established, first one time during class, and then two times during class.

RESULTS

Table 9.2 presents data reflecting the number of homework problems completed by Niki and the frequency with which she raised her hand.

CONCLUSION

The data appeared to suggest that goal setting was effective in motivating Niki to complete her homework assignments and to increase the frequency of her participation in class. Although Niki didn't consistently volunteer answers at the goal set (two times each class), she disclosed to Ms. Morton that this was because she didn't want to appear like she was trying to be the "teacher's pet" or trying to be a "math whiz." Niki did, however, express that finishing her homework made her feel confident that she could volunteer a correct answer or respond if called upon and that made the class a lot more enjoyable.

Table 9.2

	Baseline Homework (No. Problems)	Homework with Goals (No. Problems)	Volunteering Baseline (Frequency)	Volunteering with Goals (Frequency)
Day 1	2 of 10		0	
Day 2	1 of 10		0	
Day 3	1 of 10		0	
Day 4	0 of 10		0	
Day 5		3 of 10	0	
Day 6		6 of 10	0	
Day 7		10 of 10	0	
Day 8		10 of 10	0	
Day 9		9 of 10		1
Day 10		10 of 10		1
Day 11		10 of 10		1
Day 12		10 of 10		1
Day 13		10 of 10		2
Day 14		10 of 10		1

Action Research

Improving Use of Grammar Elements in Story Writing

A n interesting application of the multiple baseline design was reported by Graham and Harris (1989). A teacher as action researcher used a multiple-baseline design to test a self-monitoring strategy to improve a student's use of six grammar elements in story writing.

Baseline

Prior to implementing the intervention, baseline data were collected simultaneously on the student's use of six elements: main character, locale, goal, reaction, time of story, and ending. For each element present, a score of 1 was assigned, and if considered highly developed, a score of 2 would be assigned. The factors were paired, so for each pairing a score could range from 0 to 4.

Intervention

The intervention entailed teaching the student how to graph the occurrence of these elements within her writing. After a stable baseline was obtained, the student was instructed to monitor (graph) the pres-

ence of the first paired elements (i.e., main character and locale). The student then began to monitor the inclusion of goal and reaction elements (in Step 2) and finally, time of story and ending (in Step 3).

Data Presentation

Figure 9.2 provides the data reflecting the percentage of correct responses for each set of words. It is evident that improvement occurred only when the treatment was introduced for that set of writing elements.

Conclusions

In reviewing the graphs, it appears that self-monitoring by graphing led to some improvement in the student's use of the story elements. Monitoring appeared to facilitate the student's use of main character, locale, goal, and reaction elements within her writing. However, the gains were modest, and the teacher may decide to incorporate other strategies besides self-monitoring to improve the student's writing.

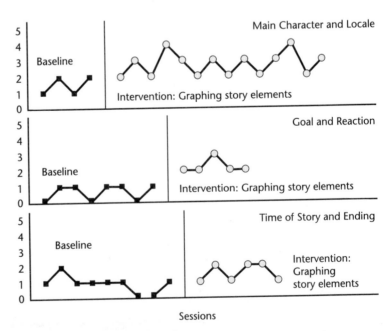

Figure 9.2 *Multiple baselines: Number of instances of story elements*

Source: Adapted from Graham & Harris (1989)

COOPERATIVE LEARNING EXERCISE

Designing for Multiple Treatments

Directions

Below you will find a description of an action research project developed by an eighth-grade science teacher, using a multiple baseline design. With a colleague or classmate, discuss the questions.

Case Presentation

Ms. Morton is an eighth-grade science teacher who attempted to increase the motivation of her students by employing a goal-setting strategy. Ms. Morton identified three students in her fifth period who demonstrated low levels of involvement in class participation. She kept records of how often each of these three students raised their hands in an attempt to volunteer an answer. Next, she selected one of the students as her target, and each day she asked that student to predict how many questions he would be able to answer in that day's class. For the next week, she continued to count the number of times each of the three students volunteered answers. In the third week of her action research project she selected one of the two remaining students and introduced the daily goal-setting strategy with that student, while continuing it with the first. Again, data were collected on all three students' hand raising. In the fourth week she introduced the goal setting to the final student and continued that process with all three students for another week, still collecting data on hand raising.

Questions for Reflection

1. What are your feelings about the teacher's use of "hand raising to volunteer answers" as her measure of motivation? What would you use in addition to, or as a substitute for, this variable?

2. The teacher used a multiple baseline strategy, assuming that the goal-setting strategy was effective in having the student(s) volunteer answers. Develop a graph to demonstrate that effectiveness.

3. How would you have assigned each student to "treatment"?

4. Why would a multiple baseline design be preferable to a reversal design in this situation?

5. Assuming that the data demonstrated that the goal-setting strategy increased student motivation, what do you think the teacher should do next? Why?

INDIVIDUAL GUIDED PRACTICE EXERCISE

Single Subject, Multiple Treatments

Directions

The information on motivation presented in this chapter suggested that two variables, value and expectancy, are important to increasing motivation, including the motivation to achieve. The following exercise is designed to assist you in identifying a number of strategies useful in increasing your perceived value of a learning activity as well as increasing your own expectancy of success.

Step 1 Identify one course or subject area for which you would like to increase the time you devote to studying.

Step 2 For a period of one week (seven days) make a daily record of the number of minutes spent studying that material.

Step 3 Treatment 1—Goal Setting

For the next seven days, prior to studying, set a goal for the amount of time you will spend studying. Attempt to keep the goal realistic and achievable. After you establish the goal, set an alarm for that length of time and begin studying. The goals can vary from day to day. As with Step 2, maintain a daily record of time spent studying.

Step 4 Treatment 2—Finding Value

Identify the reason you are in school. What is it that you hope to be able to do some day? What do you want to do upon graduation? Be specific. If it is teaching, develop a mental image of yourself as a teacher. If you are interested in going into sales, imagine what your life will look like once you are a successful businessperson.

Now, for the next seven days, continue setting study-time goals as done in the previous step. However, in addition to goal setting, take one minute before beginning your studying to close your eyes, visualize your ultimate goal and how your life will be when you graduate, and then mentally repeat to yourself: "Each time I study, I get closer to successfully achieving my goal of being a successful (fill in the blank)."

As with the previous steps, maintain a daily record of time spent studying.

Step 5 Data

Graph the data collected for each day of the experiment.

Step 6   Analysis

    1. Was your baseline stable (for the first seven days)?

    2. Was there an elevation with treatment 1?

    3. Was there an elevation over treatment 1 when treatment 2 was added?

Step 7   Reflections

    How would you explain your data? Do they support the hypothesized treatment effects? What threats to internal validity existed? What could you do to improve this study?

Connections

FOCUS

The current Connections section has a twofold objective. First, it is hoped that this activity will help you to identify strategies considered effective in raising the motivation of the underachieving student. Second, it is hoped that you will be able to engage in a collaborative relationship with a classroom teacher in order to test the effectiveness of these strategies.

DIRECTIONS

    1. Go to the following Web site:

       http://www.teachers.net

       Pose the following question in a chat room or post it on a bulletin board:

       Message: "I am interested in learning how to increase student motivation to achieve. What specific strategies have you found effective in helping the underachieving child to see the *value* of your specific learning activity?"

    2. Review the suggested strategies and select three that you feel have special merit.

    3. Design an action research project using a multiple baseline design and three different treatments (the three suggestions provided in Step 2). Invite one of the teachers who provided the suggestions to consider implementing your project, or if you have access to a small group of students or another cooperative teacher, try out the project with that group.

◆ Key Terms

achievement need	multiple baseline	self-efficacy
expectancy	need	stable baseline
learning goals	reversal design	value

◆ Suggested Readings

Barlow, D. H., & Hersen, M. (1984). *Single case experimental design: Strategies for studying behavior change* (2nd ed.). Tarrytown, NY: Pergamon Press.

Neuman, S. B., & McCormick, S. (Eds.). (1995). *Single-subject experimental research: Applications for literacy.* Newark, DE: International Reading Association.

Pintrich, P., & Schunk, D. (1996). *Motivation in education: Theory, research and applications.* Upper Saddle River, NJ: Prentice-Hall.

◆ References

Alschuler, A., Tabor, D., & McIntyre, J. (1971). *Teaching achievement motivation.* Middletown, CT: Educational Ventures.

Atkinson, J. (1980). Motivational effects in so-called tests of ability and educational achievement. In L. Fyans (Ed.), *Achievement motivation: Recent trends in theory and research.* New York: Plenum.

———. (1983). *Personality, motivation and action.* New York: Praeger.

Baer, D. M., Wolf, M. M., & Risley, T. R. (1968). Some current dimensions of applied behavior analysis. *Journal of Applied Behavior Analysis, 1*(1), 91–97.

Bandura, A. (1982). Self-efficacy mechanisms in human agency. *American Psychologist, 37*(2), 122–147.

———. (1993). Perceived self-efficacy in cognitive development and functioning. *Educational Psychologist, 28*(2), 117–148.

———, & Schunk, D. (1981). Cultivating competence, self-efficacy, and intrinsic interest through proximal self-motivation. *Journal of Personality and Social Psychology, 41,* 586–598.

Barlow, D. H., & Hersen, M. (1984). *Single case experimental design: Strategies for studying behavior change* (2nd ed.). Tarrytown, NY: Pergamon Press.

Bruning, R., Schraw, G., & Ronning, R. (1995). *Cognitive psychology and instruction* (2nd ed.). Upper Saddle River, NJ: Prentice-Hall.

Campbell, D. T., & Stanley, J. C. (1963). *Experimental and quasi-experimental designs for research.* Chicago: Rand McNally.

Eccles, J. (1987). Gender roles and women's achievement-related decisions. *Psychology of Women Quarterly, 11*(2), 135–172.

Eshel, Y., & Klein, Z. (1981). Development of academic self-concept of lower-class and middle-class primary school children. *Journal of Educational Psychology, 73,* 287–293.

Feather, N. (Ed.). (1982). *Expectations and actions.* Hillsdale, NJ: Erlbaum.

Graham, S., & Harris, K. R. (1989). Improving learning disabled students' skills at composing essays: Self-instructional strategy training. *Exceptional Children, 56*(3), 201–214.

Kukla, A. (1972). Attributional determinants of achievement-related behavior. *Journal of Personality and Social Psychology, 21*(2), 166–174.

Locke, E., & Latham, G. (1990). *A theory of goal setting and performance.* Upper Saddle River, NJ: Prentice-Hall.

Maehr, D., & Sjogren, D. (1978). Atkinson's theory of achievement motivation: First step toward a theory of academic motivation? *Review of Educational Research, 41*(2), 143–161.

McClelland, D. (1985). *Human motivation.* Glenview, IL: Scott, Foresman.

Nicholls, J. (Ed.). (1984). *The development of achievement motivation.* Greenwich, CT: JAI Press.

Pintrich, P., & Garcia, T. (1991). Student goal orientation and self-regulation in the college classroom. Pp. 371–402 in M. Maehr & P. Pintrich (Eds.), *Advances in motivation and achievement* (Vol. 7). Greenwich, CT: JAI Press.

Pintrich, P., & Schunk, D. (1996). *Motivation in education: Theory, research and applications.* Upper Saddle River, NJ: Prentice-Hall.

Ridley, D., McCombs, B., & Taylor, K. (1994). Walking the talk: Fostering self-regulated learning in the classroom. *Middle School Journal, 26*(2), 52–57.

Schunk, D. (1990). *Perceptions of efficacy and classroom motivation.* Paper presented at annual meeting of the American Educational Research Association (Boston, April).

Schunk, D. H. (1995). Self-efficacy and education and instruction. In J. E. Maddus (Ed.), *Self-efficacy, adaptation, and adjustment.* New York: Plenum.

Stipek, D. (1996). Motivation and instruction. Pp. 85–113 in D. Berliner & R. Calfee (Eds.), *Handbook of Educational Psychology.* New York: Macmillan.

Tollefson, N., Tracy, D., Johnsen, E., Farmer, W., & Buenning, M. (1984). Goal setting and personal responsibility for LD adolescents. *Psychology in the Schools, 21*(2), 224–233.

BECOMING
AN ACTION
RESEARCHER

CHAPTER 10

Becoming an Action Researcher

ractice, practice, practice!

There is a story about a young boy who is a bit lost, walking around the streets of New York City carrying a violin case and looking for Carnegie Hall. With a sense of frustration and a tiny bit of trepidation he approaches a man standing on the corner and asks, "Excuse me, sir, could you tell me how to get to Carnegie Hall?" The man turns and, after taking a moment to assess the youth and his question, clears his throat and states, "Practice, practice, practice!"

Perhaps by this point of the text you too are feeling a bit frustrated with all the new terms, concepts, and challenges. Perhaps you, like the youth in our story, know your intended destination but still feel in a bit of a quandary about how to get there. Under these conditions, the advice of the New York City helper may apply: practice, practice, practice.

Action research is about practice! It is about approaching professional decision making with the mind-set and the skills of a researcher. The flavor, the richness, the value of action research can only truly be known by experience, by doing. This chapter is structured to provide you with the vicarious experience of one teacher as action researcher and the guided practice of your own experience as action researcher.

◆ Chapter Objectives

The intent of this chapter is to help move you from being a reader of action research to becoming a doer of action research and to provide a model and case illustration intended to guide you in the process.

After reading this chapter, you should be able to do the following:

1 Describe the steps of initiating, implementing, and utilizing action research within a practice setting.

2 Explain the applications of these action research steps as they apply to a case illustration.

3 Apply the steps needed to formulate, implement, and interpret an action research project within the domain of your current professional practice.

CONTENT MAP 10

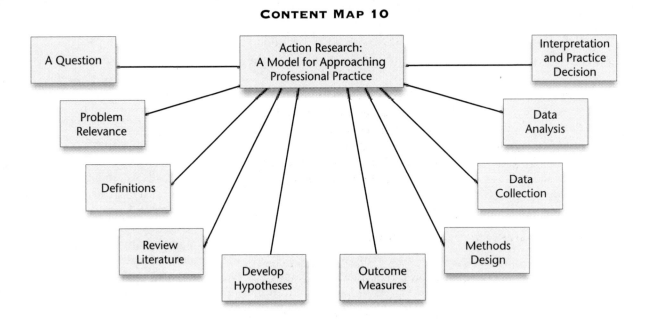

ACTION RESEARCH: A MODEL FOR APPROACHING PROFESSIONAL PRACTICE

The classic model of action research combines research and action to increase understanding and generate change. As stated throughout this text, action research is the orderly process of collecting data about a system relative to a goal or need of that system (Aguinis, 1994). The data are not arbitrary, and like other applications of the scientific method, action research is guided by hypotheses and assumptions about the phenomenon under investigation. Unlike other uses of the scientific method, the purpose differs in that knowledge alone is not the goal, but rather the goal and process of action research involve data collection that is fed back into the system with action taken as a consequence (Aguinis, 1994). Action research is a systematic, ongoing process of stating hypotheses, collecting data, and feeding the data back into the system in a process of hypothesis testing and problem solving.

Elliott (1991) describes the process of an **action research spiral** in which the researcher

1. selects the general area and decides on his or her first action.

2. takes the action as well as monitors it.

3. examines the information collected.

4. evaluates both the process and outcomes.

5. plans the next action.

6. takes the action.

7. returns to Step 1.

So, even though action research is described as a process involving clear, distinct, linear steps, the reality is that action research is a dynamic process of moving back and forth across these steps as the data acquired continually reshape practice decisions, additional questions, and the gathering of additional data. The steps employed will be discussed and applied in the remainder of the chapter and are presented in Figure 10.1.

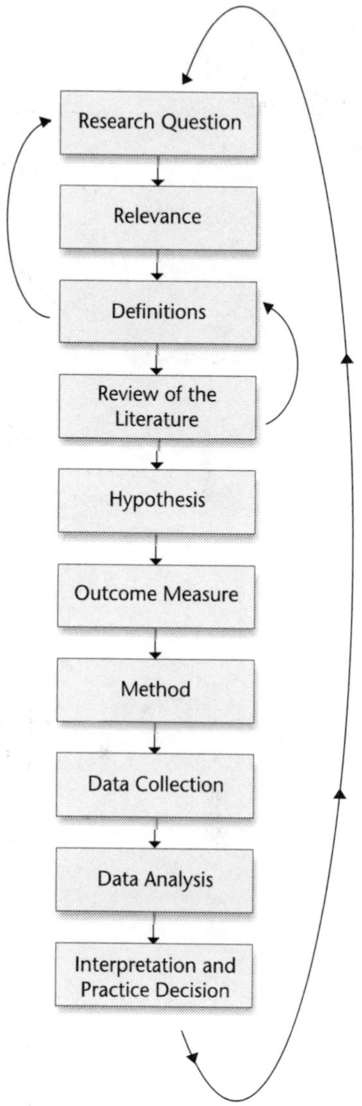

◆ Step 1: A Question, a Problem?

The first step in the action research process is the identification of the **research question.** Three types of questions seem to emerge. First, what are our teaching decisions? Second, what specifically about our teaching is effective? Finally, what can we do to enhance our effectiveness as teachers?

With these three questions as our guides for reviewing teaching effectiveness, we may soon discover an area of concern or one of simple interest. This becomes the basis of a research question or problem for investigation.

◆ Step 2: Problem Relevance, Problem Significance

The action researcher needs to develop not only a statement of the research problem, but also a description of the background of the problem, including the factors that caused it to become a problem in the first place. The goal is to answer questions such as: "Why study it?" "What do I expect will happen as a result of this investigation?" "How is the problem and the study significant to my teaching?"

◆ Step 3: Definitions

Up to this point, the area of concern may have been identified and described with vague generalities or global descriptions. In this third step, the action researcher begins to identify and define in more concrete terms the concepts, the constructs, and the variables involved. When possible, the action researcher defines these by actions or operations performed (i.e., **operational definitions**).

Figure 10.1 *Action research flow chart*

◆ Step 4: Review of Related Literature

Though the problem under investigation is somewhat unique to one action researcher, it is possible that others have encountered similar problems or concerns. Further, it is possible that other individuals have made discoveries that could be of use to the action researcher. Therefore, reviewing the professional literature for evidence of those discoveries may prove to be a valuable step in intervention planning.

◆ Step 5: Developing Hypotheses

As noted previously, the intent of action research is to effect change. Therefore, the action researcher attempts to articulate the change anticipated and the conditions under which that change should occur. The **hypothesis** is simply a predictive statement of what will happen when the action researcher institutes a change in teaching practice. Having a formulated hypothesis helps the action researcher develop methods and measures for assessing the accuracy of the prediction. Knowing where we would like to go can help in planning how to get there.

Within the action research model, hypotheses are truly "works in progress." As data are collected and decisions are made, the hypothesis may be reshaped. In addition, a new hypothesis may emerge from the data as the study progresses.

◆ Step 6: Outcome Measures

As action researchers seek to increase their understanding of the impact of specific teaching decisions, measurement of those decisions and their impact needs to be recorded. There is no one clear prescription for the type of measurement or data to be employed (e.g., quantitative only, qualitative, combined, etc.). On the contrary, a variety of data types should be collected to capture the complexity of reality (Alderfer & Brown, 1975; Aguinis, 1994; Argyris et al., 1985). The action researcher should use outcome assessment, which measures change from multiple perspectives (i.e., the student, the teacher-researcher, and others) and through multiple approaches.

◆ Step 7: Methods—Creating a Design

As with any study, in order for conclusions to be considered valid, the researcher must consider the use of a **design** that provides accurate data collection and interpretation. The action researcher must determine how the research questions can best be addressed. Are qualitative methods such as case studies or participant observations with extensive field notes best suited for the research questions, or would a form of baseline design or reversal or time series with the focus on change over time be more appropriate? Should these two types of data be combined in a planned, meaningful way in order to test the hypothesis?

◆ Step 8: Data Collection

The types of data the action researcher chooses to collect, as well as the method employed in collecting these data, will be influenced not only by the nature of the problem but also the interest and talents of the researcher and the demands and opportunities provided by the situation. However, the information gathered must be as detailed and as informative as possible. It is important that the methods employed be as valid as possible while at the same time not intruding on or distorting teaching practice. Action researchers need to remember that they are teachers as well as researchers and that they have a professional responsibility to their students.

◆ Step 9: Data Analysis

Teachers often shy away from data analysis, viewing it as requiring special statistical knowledge and competency. **Data analysis** is fundamental to understanding the experience of the research. At a minimum, the data need to be organized and grouped with themes, with trends and characteristics noted. When appropriate, action researchers should use visual presentation and descriptive and inferential statistics.

◆ Step 10: Interpretation and Practice Decisions

A keystone of action research lies in its link with practice decisions—an applied outcome. In reviewing the data, the teacher as action researcher balances **research significance** with **practical relevance.** Having answered the question What happens if . . . ?, the action researcher can then answer questions such as What does knowing what happens mean to my students? To me? To my professional decision making or to my current teaching?

PUTTING IT ALL TOGETHER

What follows is a case illustration of the development, implementation, analysis, and application of action research in a middle-school setting. Though the case has been presented in a linear fashion, moving sequentially from problem identification through design, analysis, etc., the action research process is not linear. It is a process of recycling (as noted above), in which initial questions shape data collection, which in turn modifies thought and further data collection. Thus, the overly simplistic linear presentation, while providing an understandable forum for discussion, belies the reality of action research. In addition to providing the specifics of the action research process, the following case illustration includes the action researcher's thoughts to allow the reader to view the teacher's own experience as the process takes shape.

Action Research

A Case Illustration from Beginning to End: Hostility Abounds

The action researcher is a school counselor, confronted with the apparent "uncontrollable hostility" of one student, Thomas, a seventh grader.

Step 1: Research Question

Thomas was referred to the counselor by the assistant principal, who wrote the counselor stating:

> Joan, could you please spend some time with Thomas. He has become quite a handful and is increasingly getting in trouble because of his "bullying." On three separate occasions, I noticed him attempting to "bully" other children. On one occasion, I saw him actually threaten another child, stating that he would hurt him if he did not give him his lunch. I have spoken to Thomas, even tried to punish him and threatened to have him expelled, but it doesn't seem to have any impact. I am also concerned that some of the other students appear to be looking up to him as if he is some kind of role model or leader.

Researcher Reflections

- Sounds like the assistant principal feels this is urgent.
- Punishment and threats appear to have little impact.
- I wonder what is causing or maintaining this behavior in light of all the negative consequences Thomas has experienced.
- I need to be a little clearer about what has been happening (collecting data via interview).

Step 2: Relevance

The counselor gathered additional information (qualitative data) by observing Thomas interacting in the lunchroom and study hall and by conducting an open interview with Thomas.

Researcher Reflections

- I observed Thomas verbally threaten to hurt a child if he couldn't push in front of him in the lunch line.
- I observed Thomas take half a sandwich from another student as he walked past that student.
- In the interview, Thomas smiled as he stated, "I'm tough!"
- Thomas acts as if being tough and intimidating to other students is cool. He appears to take pride in how the other students "fear" him.
- Thomas explained that he is not afraid of the assistant principal and "if he wants to give me detentions or even kick me out, I could care less!"
- If this isn't curtailed soon, not only may he be removed from school, but he could also be laying the groundwork for an unhealthy, unproductive, and potentially dangerous lifestyle.

Step 3: Definitions

The counselor spoke with Thomas's homeroom teacher, who characterized him as "a sneak and a bully!" She also referred to Thomas as a "real hoodlum."

Researcher Reflections

- It would help to be more concrete in defining Thomas's behavior, labeled by the teacher as bullying or hoodlum behavior.

(continued on page 163)

(continued from page 162)

♦ I need to talk with the homeroom teacher and the assistant principal to see if we can begin to define what it is that Thomas does.

After these interviews, the following were identified as behaviors of concern (Step 3):

1. Picks on smaller children.
2. Threatens others verbally.
3. Takes things from others without their permission or knowledge.

Step 4: Review of the Literature

The action researcher went to the university library. A search on CD-ROM of the Psychological Abstracts revealed an article that discussed the existence of different types of aggression, proactive and reactive (see Dodge & Coie, 1987), in school-aged children. A number of articles provided specific interventions for the proactive (bully-type) behavior and highlighted the potential detrimental effects of using coercive power and punishment to attempt to control bully-type behavior. She found an article by Stefanich and Bell (1985) that provided a dynamic model for classroom discipline promoting responsibility and self-motivation by adopting a least-restrictive punishment philosophy. She also found a number of articles that pointed to the use of positive reinforcement for the exhibition of prosocial behaviors (e.g., Alberti, 1986; Dougherty et al., 1985) as a way of reducing bullying.

Researcher Reflections

♦ It is clear that when you employ coercive force (threat and punishment) with a bully, you not only place him within a challenged mode but also model the use of coercive power to get what you want. That seems counterproductive to me.

♦ There seems to be success with prosocial training in which cooperation and appropriate negotiating skills and problem solving are reinforced when used.

Step 5: Hypothesis

Following the brief review of the literature, the action researcher concluded that Thomas may be a proactive aggressor, controlled more by conse-

quences than by antecedent conditions. The researcher hypothesized that if this is true, introducing a contingency management plan in which his prosocial behaviors can be reinforced should help reduce his need for displaying hostile, bully-type behaviors.

Researcher Reflections

♦ I wonder if I could get Thomas's teachers to allow him some position of status or power (collect papers?) if he demonstrates evidence of being cooperative with his peers.

♦ Maybe I could simply work out a contract with Thomas and begin modifying his behavior through a contingency management contract in which I provide him with a credit certificate to the school store when he goes a day without a discipline referral.

Step 6: Outcome Measures

Because data existed that reflected the frequency with which Thomas was sent to the disciplinarian for demonstrating one of the three identified bullying behaviors, the action researcher felt that "referral to discipline" could be used as a comparative measure of outcome. It was hypothesized that discipline referrals would decline following the introduction of a behavioral contract system. (Return to Step 5.)

Researcher Reflections

♦ I need to discuss this with Thomas and make sure he doesn't have a strong reaction to using discipline records for our data.

♦ I also need to check with the disciplinarian to make sure I have access to those records.

♦ I need to make sure that two weeks of data is sufficient and that it provides a pretty stable baseline; if not, maybe I will need to extend the baseline period.

♦ Maybe I should gather other kinds of measures, like teacher reactions and observations about Thomas's attitude in class, or even Thomas's self-evaluation. No, maybe I will just start with the discipline records. I am pretty busy right now with a heavy caseload.

(continued on page 164)

(continued from page 163)

Step 7: Method

The action researcher decided to use a simple time series (AB) design, in which discipline referrals given as a direct result of aggressive behavior would be recorded for the two weeks of treatment (i.e., with the contingency contract in place), and these data would be compared with the record of referral for the two-week period before the treatment was introduced.

Researcher Reflections

◆ I need to make sure the lunchroom and study hall monitors, as well as Thomas's teachers, are not told we are doing something differently. I don't want them to change their behavior or their style of monitoring.

◆ I need to speak with Thomas and establish the contract.

Step 8: Data Collection

The data reflecting frequency of referral were collected and are listed in Table 10.1. These data include only those disciplinary referrals that came as a result of Thomas exhibiting one of the previously defined aggressive behaviors. Other disciplinary referrals, such as for smoking and cutting class, were noted but not included in the action research.

Researcher Reflections

◆ I am going to keep some anecdotal notes on teacher comments, observed behaviors, etc. These may help me to understand my findings better. (Qualitative data.)

◆ Thomas hasn't been getting many payoffs. Maybe this was a bad idea. I just have to wait. It is early in the program (day 3).

◆ I'm getting the feeling that we may need something with a stronger incentive. This is day 10 and it doesn't look so great.

Step 9: Data Analysis

The data were graphed and visually inspected (see Figure 10.2)

Researcher Reflections

◆ It doesn't appear to be a big change, but maybe I didn't give it enough time.

Table 10.1   Disciplinary Referrals

Baseline		Treatment Period	
DAY	REFERRALS	DAY	REFERRALS
1	3	1	0
2	1	2	1
3	0	3	2
4	2	4	2
5	1	5	1
6	2	6	0
7	1	7	2
8	1	8	1
9	2	9	2
10	2	10	2

(continued on page 165)

(continued from page 164)

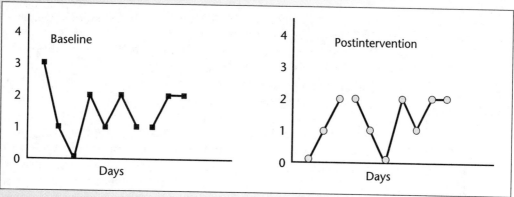

Figure 10.2 *Discipline referrals*

- He was averaging (mean) about 1.5 referrals a day during baseline and 1.3 during treatment. This doesn't seem an important improvement worth the effort (practical significance).
- I wonder how he will react to these data.

Step 10: Interpretation and Practice Decision

After "eyeballing" the data, the researcher concluded that there did not appear to be an intervention effect.

Researcher Reflections

- I wonder what happened? Maybe I didn't use the treatment long enough.
- Maybe I misread the type of aggression being exhibited by Thomas.
- Perhaps there is something else going on that I am missing.

The researcher decided to share the data with Thomas to see if further insights could be gained.

Researcher Reflections

- Thomas was very clear that the intervention wasn't working and, in fact, didn't think it would work from the beginning.

- Thomas stated that he would rather feel "powerful" and "in control" than get some silly rewards like the ones I was offering as part of the contract.
- Thomas said he enjoyed it at his other school because he sometimes was asked to do things by his teachers, and that made him feel important.
- I wonder if we re-contracted for another two-week period, but this time I will engage Thomas as an office helper (during his study hall) as the contingency if he had no incidents of bullying during the previous day. He says he would like to help out in guidance.

In discussing this modification with Thomas, he demonstrated a clear enthusiasm about the possibility of helping out (an emotion he failed to exhibit regarding the first intervention). It was decided to try the intervention again with this new contingency (practice decision). At this point, the action researcher began to recycle through the stages of the process.

INDIVIDUAL GUIDED PRACTICE EXERCISE

Applying the Model: A Guided Tour of Your Own Experience

As in each of the previous chapters, you are asked to apply what you have learned to your own current professional or personal experience. Again, it is suggested that you not only work through this exercise on your own, but that you share your conclusions, your insights, and your experience with a colleague or a mentor in order to benefit from the insight and experience of another.

For each step of the action research process, questions are presented to stimulate your thinking and the development of your action research project. The questions listed are not intended to be exhaustive or exclusive. They are simply initial stimulants to the development of an action research project. This exercise is designed to provide you with the real-life experience of "putting it all together" and give you new insights leading to more effective practice decisions.

◆ Step 1: Research Question

Take a moment and reflect on your current work situation. Name three things that you do with some regularity. Why? What else could you do?

◆ Step 2: Relevance

Of the things you identified in Step 1, which holds special importance or relevance to you and to your goals as a professional? Of the three things, which is the one thing that seems or appears least enjoyable or least effective? If changed to be more effective, which would benefit you or those with whom you work the most? Which, if changed, would have the biggest positive impact on you and your students?

◆ Step 3: Definitions

Referring to Step 2, provide observable behavioral examples when discussing "what you do" and its "impact." Be concrete, specific, and as operational as possible in your definition.

◆ Step 4: Review of the Literature

Go to the library or check resource books that have information on the same type of work or personal experience that you identified above. Investigate what others have said or done in this situation. Write down three things that others have done. Which behavior is different than what you do or have done? Which behaviors appear to be possible for you to do?

◆ Step 5: Hypothesis

Make a prediction about what may happen if you select to do the one thing you identified in Step 4. How might it affect you? How might it change or affect those with whom you work? Develop a stated hypothesis that follows the formula: "After doing (implementing) _____, I will note the following effects (outcomes): _____."

◆ Step 6: Method

How, when, and where do you plan to introduce your intervention? How and when do you intend to assess the outcome? How often will you assess the outcome? How will you be able to interpret your data? Do you need or have a point of comparison? How will you try to control for threats to validity?

Write out the specific steps you intend to take in as much detail and with as much clarity as possible. Imagine that you are writing instructions for the assembly of some item (provide Step 1, 2, etc.).

◆ Step 7: Data Collection

What instruments and methods will you use to gather data? What data will you collect? Are they qualitative data? If so, have you considered how you will organize it, or will you allow categories to simply emerge? Will you use quantitative data? What will you do with these numbers? How long will you gather data?

◆ Step 8: Data Analysis

Have you categorized your qualitative data? Do you see themes, trends, or consistent patterns? Will you employ descriptive statistics for your quantitative data? What do they indicate? Have you graphed them? Have you listed your data?

◆ Step 9: Interpretation and Practice Decisions

What is the research significance of your findings? Is that important? What is the practical significance of your findings? What did you learn about your practice decisions and the experience of action research? What will you do with this new knowledge? Will you make changes in your practice? Will you assess these changes further? What is valuable from your experience that should be shared with others?

Connections

This chapter focused on furthering the reader's understanding of the process of action research and applying it in a real-life teaching situation. To further assimilate this information, it may be helpful to apply the model as reflected in Figure 10.1 to other teachers' action research.

Go to the Classroom Connect Web site:

http://www.connectedteacher.com/home.asp

On the message board, post the steps involved in the action research process as listed in Figure 10.1. Ask teachers to send you examples of how they have employed action research in their classroom, and ask them to identify the degree to which they used a model similar to that listed in Figure 10.1.

Reflections: Did the teachers follow such a flow to their action research? Did they skip steps? If so, what was the impact? Was there something they could have done that would have improved their action research? Do they give evidence that some of the steps are more or less important than others?

Share your findings with your colleagues or classmates.

◆ Key Terms

action research spiral
data analysis
design

hypothesis
operational definitions
practical relevance

research question
research significance

◆ Suggested Readings

Ketterer, R., Price, R., & Politser, R. (1980). The action research paradigm. In R. Price & R. Politser (Eds.), *Evaluation and action in the social environment.* New York: Academic Press.

McLean, J. E. (1997). Teacher empowerment through action research. *Kappa Delta Pi Record, 34*(1), 34–38.

McNiff, J., Whitehead, J., & Lomax, P. (1996). *You and your action research project.* London: Routledge.

Quigley, B. A., & Kuhne, G. W. (Eds.). (1997). *Creating practical knowledge through action research.* San Francisco: Jossey-Bass.

Zuber-Skerritt, O. (Ed.). (1991). *Action research for change and development.* Brookfield, VT: Avebury.

♦ References

Alberti, R. E. (1986). *Making yourself heard: A guide to assertive relationships* (Cassette recording nos. 29532, 29533). New York: BMA Audio Cassettes.

Aguinis, H. (1994). Action research and scientific method: Presumed discrepancies and actual similarities. *Journal of Applied Behavioral Science, 29*(4), 416–431.

Alderfer, C. P., & Brown, L. D. (1975). *Learning from changing*. Beverly Hills, CA: Sage.

Argyris, C., Putman, R., & Smith, D. M. (1985). *Action science*. San Francisco: Jossey-Bass.

Dodge, K. A., & Coie, J. D. (1987). Social-information processing factors in reactive and proactive aggression in children's peer groups. *Journal of Personality and Social Psychology, 53*(6), 1146–1158.

Dougherty, B. S., Fowler, S. A., & Paine, S. C. (1985). The use of peer monitors to reduce negative interaction during recess. *Journal of Applied Behavior Analysis, 18*(2), 141–153.

Elliott, J. (1991). *Action research for educational change*. Philadelphia: Open University Press.

Stefanich, G. P., & Bell, L. C. (1985). A dynamic model for classroom discipline. *NASSP Bulletin, 69*, 19–25.

hew! Glad that's over.

Well, not quite. The text is complete and perhaps the course or the professional development experience in which you were engaged is coming to a close. Your development as an action researcher, however, is not over . . . it has just begun! The integration of research into practice needs to be a primary objective for all professional educators.

As a professional, your duties demand that you provide your students with the most effective and efficient professional practice. It is your ethical responsibility. Approaching your classroom with the skills and mind-set of a researcher will help ensure the efficacy of your teaching. In addition to becoming sophisticated consumers of research and maintaining your knowledge and awareness of the latest findings and standards of practice, you need to integrate research into your teaching decisions—not just as content derived from studies done by others, but as a method of practice.

Action research cannot be simply read or experienced as a text or a course. Action research needs to be integrated throughout your ongoing professional development and serve as an integral part of your approach to teaching. What is needed is ownership and your active involvement as an action researcher. It is important to move action research from your head to the heart of your practice and engage in the process. We encourage you to continue to reach out, test, and share your ideas with other colleagues.

Throughout the chapters, a number of Web sites have been mentioned that provide a forum for interaction and dialogue with other professionals. In addition to those found within the chapters, the following sites may help your continued development as an effective teacher and action researcher.

http://www.ael.org

http://gopher.dial0in.nw.dc.us

Over? Not quite! It has just begun, and that can be very exciting.

INDEX

ABAB research design. *See* reversal (ABAB) design
AB research design. *See* two-phase (AB) design
accommodation, 37, 39, 40
accountability, desire for, 6, 8
achievement need, 143–144
action research
    characteristics of, 5–6, 7–8
    defined, 4, 158
    as an ethical responsibility, 8
    examples of, 10, 23, 41, 64–65, 84, 100, 118, 132, 148, 162–165
    exploring, Web site for, 25
    focus of, 22
    heart of, 3
    and importance of practice, 157
    multiple benefits of, 6–7
    origin of, 7
    personalizing, exercise in, 25
    reasons for using, 8
    searching online for, 12
    targeting areas for, exercise in, 11–12
    use of, rise in, 4–5
    uses for, 6, 8
action researchers
    becoming, 6, 11, 23, 157–168
    defining, 4
    primary concern of, 9–10
action research model, 158–161
action research process
    applying, exercise in, 166–167
    case illustration of, 162–165
    cyclical nature of, 8–9
    as dynamic, 48, 158–159
    exploring, Web site for, 168
    flow chart of, 159
    steps employed in, 159–161
action research spiral, 158–159
actions, impact of, 7
action steps, developing and implementing, 8
adaptation
    concept of, in Piaget's theory, 36–37, 39
    of theory and practice, 3
adolescent identity, 63

advance organizers, 124, 130–131, 144
    exploring, Web site for, 134
    testing effectiveness of, exercise in, 131–133
aggression
        See also hostility
    and class climate, 18–19
    and modeling, exploring, Web site for, 121
    outbursts of, study on, validity of, 77–82
Alta Vista Web site, 12
alternative explanations
    elimination of, 22, 82
    plausibility of, reducing, 125
anxiety, 59
application
    emphasis on, 10
    example of, 23
applied outcome, 161
applied research, defined, 4
assimilation, 36–37, 39, 40
auditory modality, 102
Ausubel, David, 124, 130
autonomy
    and constructivist teaching, 129
    researching, 61
    versus shame and doubt, 60

Bandura, Albert, 117, 144
baseline, defined, 94
baseline data
        See also pretesting
    in multiple baseline design, 139, 140, 141, 145, 148
    in reversal (ABAB) design, 125–127
    stability of, 94, 95–96, 109, 111
    in two-phase (AB) design, 111–112, 113, 118, 164, 165
    within-subject designs and, 94, 95–96, 99
basic trust, 59
behavior, indicating degree of, 56
behavioral observation, training in, 32
behavior patterns, describing, 57
Bruner, Jerome, 129
bullying, 162–165
        See also aggression